Math Expressions

Volume 2

Homework and Remembering

Developed by
The Children's Math Worlds
Research Project

PROJECT DIRECTOR AND AUTHOR
Dr. Karen C. Fuson

This material is based upon work supported by the
National Science Foundation
under Grant Numbers
ESI-9816320, REC-9806020, and RED-935373.

Any opinions, findings, and conclusions or recommendations expressed in this material are those of the author and do not necessarily reflect the views of the National Science Foundation.

HOUGHTON MIFFLIN BOSTON

Teacher Reviewers

Kindergarten
Patricia Stroh Sugiyama
Wilmette, Illinois

Barbara Wahle
Evanston, Illinois

Grade 1
Sandra Budson
Newton, Massachusetts

Janet Pecci
Chicago, Illinois

Megan Rees
Chicago, Illinois

Grade 2
Molly Dunn
Danvers, Massachusetts

Agnes Lesnick
Hillside, Illinois

Rita Soto
Chicago, Illinois

Grade 3
Jane Curran
Honesdale, Pennsylvania

Sandra Tucker
Chicago, Illinois

Grade 4
Sara Stoneberg Llibre
Chicago, Illinois

Sheri Roedel
Chicago, Illinois

Grade 5
Todd Atler
Chicago, Illinois

Leah Barry
Norfolk, Massachusetts

Credits

Cover art: (scale) © HMCo./Richard Hutchings. (elephant) © Art Wolfe/Stone/Getty Images. (chipmunk) © David W. Hamilton/The Image Bank/Getty Images.

Illustrative art: Robin Boyer/Deborah Wolfe, LTD
Technical art: Nesbitt Graphics, Inc.
Photos: Nesbitt Graphics, Inc.

Copyright © 2006 by Houghton Mifflin Company. All rights reserved.

No part of this work may be reproduced or transmitted in any form or by any means, electronic or mechanical, including photocopying or recording, or by any information storage or retrieval system without the prior written permission of the copyright owner unless such copying is expressly permitted by federal copyright law. With the exception of nonprofit transcription into Braille, Houghton Mifflin is not authorized to grant permission for further uses of this work. Permission must be obtained from the individual copyright owner as identified herein. Address requests for permission to make copies of Houghton Mifflin material to School Permissions, Houghton Mifflin Company, 222 Berkeley Street, Boston, MA 02116.

Printed in the U.S.A.

ISBN-13: 978-0-618-64116-1
ISBN-10: 0-618-64116-5

7 8 9 1421 11 10
4500234672

4-3 Homework

Home Study Sheet A

5s

Count-bys	Mixed Up ×	Mixed Up ÷
1 × 5 = 5	2 × 5 = 10	10 ÷ 5 = 2
2 × 5 = 10	9 × 5 = 45	35 ÷ 5 = 7
3 × 5 = 15	1 × 5 = 5	50 ÷ 5 = 10
4 × 5 = 20	5 × 5 = 25	5 ÷ 5 = 1
5 × 5 = 25	7 × 5 = 35	20 ÷ 5 = 4
6 × 5 = 30	3 × 5 = 15	15 ÷ 5 = 3
7 × 5 = 35	10 × 5 = 50	30 ÷ 5 = 6
8 × 5 = 40	6 × 5 = 30	40 ÷ 5 = 8
9 × 5 = 45	4 × 5 = 20	25 ÷ 5 = 5
10 × 5 = 50	8 × 5 = 40	45 ÷ 5 = 9

2s

Count-bys	Mixed Up ×	Mixed Up ÷
1 × 2 = 2	7 × 2 = 14	20 ÷ 2 = 10
2 × 2 = 4	1 × 2 = 2	2 ÷ 2 = 1
3 × 2 = 6	3 × 2 = 6	6 ÷ 2 = 3
4 × 2 = 8	5 × 2 = 10	16 ÷ 2 = 8
5 × 2 = 10	6 × 2 = 12	12 ÷ 2 = 6
6 × 2 = 12	8 × 2 = 16	4 ÷ 2 = 2
7 × 2 = 14	2 × 2 = 4	10 ÷ 2 = 5
8 × 2 = 16	10 × 2 = 20	8 ÷ 2 = 4
9 × 2 = 18	4 × 2 = 8	14 ÷ 2 = 7
10 × 2 = 20	9 × 2 = 18	18 ÷ 2 = 9

10s

Count-bys	Mixed Up ×	Mixed Up ÷
1 × 10 = 10	1 × 10 = 10	80 ÷ 10 = 8
2 × 10 = 20	5 × 10 = 50	10 ÷ 10 = 1
3 × 10 = 30	2 × 10 = 20	50 ÷ 10 = 5
4 × 10 = 40	8 × 10 = 80	90 ÷ 10 = 9
5 × 10 = 50	7 × 10 = 70	40 ÷ 10 = 4
6 × 10 = 60	3 × 10 = 30	100 ÷ 10 = 10
7 × 10 = 70	4 × 10 = 40	30 ÷ 10 = 3
8 × 10 = 80	6 × 10 = 60	20 ÷ 10 = 2
9 × 10 = 90	10 × 10 = 100	70 ÷ 10 = 7
10 × 10 = 100	9 × 10 = 90	60 ÷ 10 = 6

9s

Count-bys	Mixed Up ×	Mixed Up ÷
1 × 9 = 9	2 × 9 = 18	81 ÷ 9 = 9
2 × 9 = 18	4 × 9 = 36	18 ÷ 9 = 2
3 × 9 = 27	7 × 9 = 63	36 ÷ 9 = 4
4 × 9 = 36	8 × 9 = 72	9 ÷ 9 = 1
5 × 9 = 45	3 × 9 = 27	54 ÷ 9 = 6
6 × 9 = 54	10 × 9 = 90	27 ÷ 9 = 3
7 × 9 = 63	1 × 9 = 9	63 ÷ 9 = 7
8 × 9 = 72	6 × 9 = 54	72 ÷ 9 = 8
9 × 9 = 81	5 × 9 = 45	90 ÷ 9 = 10
10 × 9 = 90	9 × 9 = 81	45 ÷ 9 = 5

4-3 Homework

Name _____ Date _____

Home Signature Sheet

	Count-Bys Homework Helper	Multiplications Homework Helper	Divisions Homework Helper
0			
1			
2			
3			
4			
5			
6			
7			
8			
9			
10			

4-4 Homework

Name

Date

Use this chart to practice your 5s count-bys, multiplications, and divisions. Then have your Homework Helper test you.

	In Order ×	Mixed Up ×	Mixed Up ÷
5s	1 × 5 = 5	4 × 5 = 20	20 ÷ 5 = 4
	2 × 5 = 10	7 × 5 = 35	5 ÷ 5 = 1
	3 × 5 = 15	2 × 5 = 10	50 ÷ 5 = 10
	4 × 5 = 20	5 × 5 = 25	35 ÷ 5 = 7
	5 × 5 = 25	9 × 5 = 45	15 ÷ 5 = 3
	6 × 5 = 30	1 × 5 = 5	45 ÷ 5 = 9
	7 × 5 = 35	10 × 5 = 50	10 ÷ 5 = 2
	8 × 5 = 40	3 × 5 = 15	25 ÷ 5 = 5
	9 × 5 = 45	6 × 5 = 30	40 ÷ 5 = 8
	10 × 5 = 50	8 × 5 = 40	30 ÷ 5 = 6

UNIT 4 LESSON 4

The Meaning of Division

4-4 Homework

Multiply or divide to find the missing numbers. Then check your answers at the bottom of this page.

1. $5 \times 6 = \square$
2. $45 \div 5 = \square$
3. $5 \times \square = 35$

4. $\square \times 5 = 10$
5. $3 \times 5 = \square$
6. $50 / 5 = \square$

7. $5 \cdot 9 = \square$
8. $\square \cdot 5 = 20$
9. $5\overline{)25}$

10. $5 * \square = 40$
11. $5 \cdot 5 = \square$
12. $\dfrac{35}{5} = \square$

13. $5 \cdot \square = 15$
14. $30 \div 5 = \square$
15. $5 \times \square = 45$

16. $\square \div 5 = 7$
17. $\dfrac{10}{5} = \square$
18. $5 \cdot 8 = \square$

19. $5\overline{)20}$
20. $5 \times \square = 5$
21. $5 \times \square = 50$

Answers: 1. 30 2. 9 3. 7 4. 2 5. 15 6. 10 7. 45 8. 4 9. 5 10. 8 11. 25 12. 7 13. 3 14. 6 15. 9 16. 35 17. 2 18. 40 19. 4 20. 1 21. 10

4-4 Homework

Name _____ **Date** _____

Study Plan

Homework Helper _____

Write a multiplication equation and a division equation for each problem. Then solve the problem.

1. Mandy's Diner has a total of 20 chairs. The chairs are divided equally among 5 tables. How many chairs are at each table?

   _____

2. Tarek divided 30 nickels into 5 piles. He put the same number of nickels in each pile. How many nickels were in each pile?

   _____

3. A group of singers has 45 members. The singers are arranged in groups of 5 on the stage. How many groups are there?

   _____

4. Brianna arranged 40 marbles into an array with 5 marbles in each row. How many rows of marbles were in her array?

   _____

Show your work.

4-4 Remembering

Solve each problem. If there is not enough information to solve the problem, tell what else you would need to know.

Show your work.

1. Mona wrote 7 serious poems and some funny poems. She wrote 12 poems in all. How many funny poems did she write?

   _____

2. Lidia baked 14 cakes. She gave some cakes to her neighbors. How many cakes does Lidia have left?

   _____

Use the bar graph to solve each problem.

3. How many more stuffed animals are there than bicycles?

   _____

4. How many board games and stuffed animals are there altogether?

   _____

5. How many fewer bicycles are there than board games?

   _____

6. Write a problem using the information in the bar graph. Solve your problem.

   _____
   _____
   _____

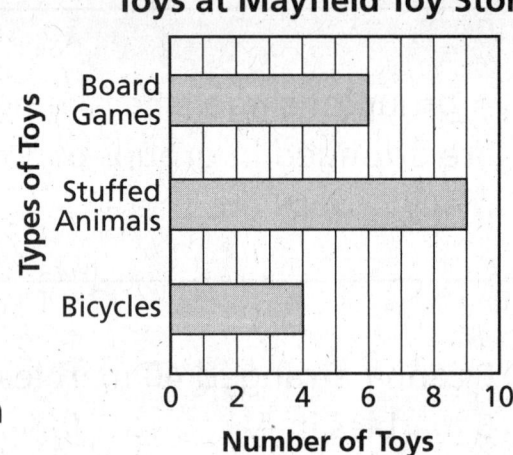

Toys at Mayfield Toy Store

116 UNIT 4 LESSON 4   The Meaning of Division

4–5 Homework

Use this chart to practice your 2s count-bys, multiplications, and divisions. Then have your Homework Helper test you.

	× In Order	× Mixed Up	÷ Mixed Up
2s	1 × 2 = 2	4 × 2 = 8	18 ÷ 2 = 9
	2 × 2 = 4	7 × 2 = 14	6 ÷ 2 = 3
	3 × 2 = 6	2 × 2 = 4	2 ÷ 2 = 1
	4 × 2 = 8	5 × 2 = 10	16 ÷ = 8
	5 × 2 = 10	9 × 2 = 18	1 ÷ 2 = 7
	6 × 2 = 12	1 × 2 = 2	4 ÷ 2 = 2
	7 × 2 = 14	10 × 2 = 20	20 ÷ 2 = 10
	8 × 2 = 16	3 × 2 =	8 ÷ 2 = 4
	9 × 2 = 18	6 × 2 12	12 ÷ 2 = 6
	10 × 2 = 20	8 × . = 16	10 ÷ 2 = 5

UNIT 4 LESSON 5

Multiply and Divide with 2

4-5 Homework

Multiply or divide to find the missing numbers. Then check your answers at the bottom of this page.

1. $2 \times 4 =$ ☐
2. $20 \div 5 =$ ☐
3. $6 * 2 =$ ☐

4. $45 / 5 =$ ☐
5. $2 \cdot 10 =$ ☐
6. $\dfrac{20}{2} =$ ☐

7. $5 \times 10 =$ ☐
8. $16 \div 2 =$ ☐
9. $6 \times 5 =$ ☐

10. $30 / 5 =$ ☐
11. $5 \cdot 7 =$ ☐
12. $2\overline{)18}$

13. $8 * 2 =$ ☐
14. $\dfrac{25}{5} =$ ☐
15. $5 \cdot 4 =$ ☐

16. $16 / 2 =$ ☐
17. $2\overline{)10}$
18. $2 * 7 =$ ☐

19. $5 \times 5 =$ ☐
20. $14 \div 2 =$ ☐
21. $\dfrac{☐}{5} = 7$

1. 8 2. 4 3. 12 4. 9 5. 20 6. 10 7. 50 8. 8 9. 30 10. 6 11. 35 12. 9 13. 16 14. 5 15. 20 16. 8 17. 5 18. 14 19. 25 20. 7 21. 35

Multiply and Divide with 2

Homework 4–5

Name _____ Date _____

Home Check Sheet 1: 5s and 2s

5s Multiplications	5s Divisions	2s Multiplications	2s Divisions
2 × 5 = 10	30 / 5 = 6	4 × 2 = 8	8 / 2 = 4
5 • 6 = 30	5 ÷ 5 = 1	2 • 8 = 16	18 ÷ 2 = 9
5 * 9 = 45	15 / 5 = 3	1 * 2 = 2	2 / 2 = 1
4 × 5 = 20	50 ÷ 5 = 10	6 × 2 = 12	16 ÷ 2 = 8
5 • 7 = 35	20 / 5 = 4	2 • 9 = 18	4 / 2 = 2
10 * 5 = 50	10 ÷ 5 = 2	2 * 2 = 4	20 ÷ 2 = 10
1 × 5 = 5	35 / 5 = 7	3 × 2 = 6	10 / 2 = 5
5 • 3 = 15	40 ÷ 5 = 8	2 • 5 = 10	12 ÷ 2 = 6
8 * 5 = 40	25 / 5 = 5	10 * 2 = 20	6 / 2 = 3
5 × 5 = 25	45 / 5 = 9	2 × 7 = 14	14 / 2 = 7
5 • 8 = 40	20 ÷ 5 = 4	2 • 10 = 20	4 ÷ 2 = 2
7 * 5 = 35	15 / 5 = 3	9 * 2 = 18	2 / 2 = 1
5 × 4 = 20	30 ÷ 5 = 6	2 × 6 = 12	8 ÷ 2 = 4
6 • 5 = 30	25 / 5 = 5	8 • 2 = 16	6 / 2 = 3
5 * 1 = 5	10 ÷ 5 = 2	2 * 3 = 6	20 ÷ 2 = 10
5 × 10 = 50	45 / 5 = 9	2 × 2 = 4	14 / 2 = 7
9 • 5 = 45	35 ÷ 5 = 7	1 • 2 = 2	10 ÷ 2 = 5
5 * 2 = 10	50 ÷ 5 = 10	2 * 4 = 8	16 ÷ 2 = 8
3 × 5 = 15	40 / 5 = 8	5 × 2 = 10	12 / 2 = 6
5 • 5 = 25	5 ÷ 5 = 1	7 • 2 = 14	18 ÷ 2 = 9

4-6 Homework

Use this chart to practice your 10s count-bys, multiplications, and divisions. Then have your Homework Helper test you.

	× In Order	× Mixed Up	÷ Mixed Up
10s	1 × 10 = 10	4 × 10 = 40	100 ÷ 10 = 10
	2 × 10 = 20	7 × 10 = 70	20 ÷ 10 = 2
	3 × 10 = 30	2 × 10 = 20	40 ÷ 10 = 4
	4 × 10 = 40	5 × 10 = 50	70 ÷ 10 = 7
	5 × 10 = 50	9 × 10 = 90	30 ÷ 10 = 3
	6 × 10 = 60	1 × 10 = 10	60 ÷ 10 = 6
	7 × 10 = 70	10 × 10 = 100	80 ÷ 10 = 8
	8 × 10 = 80	3 × 10 = 30	10 ÷ 10 = 1
	9 × 10 = 90	6 × 10 = 60	50 ÷ 10 = 5
	10 × 10 = 100	8 × 10 = 80	90 ÷ 10 = 9

4-6 Homework

Multiply or divide to find the missing numbers. Then check your answers at the bottom of this page.

1. $2 \times 10 = \square$
2. $15 \div 5 = \square$
3. $4 * 2 = \square$

4. $80 / 10 = \square$
5. $5 \cdot \square = 40$
6. $\frac{60}{10} = \square$

7. $\square \times 5 = 30$
8. $\frac{24}{2} = \square$
9. $6 \times 10 = \square$

10. $25 / 5 = \square$
11. $10 \cdot 7 = \square$
12. $14 \div 2 = \square$

13. $9 * 2 = \square$
14. $\frac{45}{5} = \square$
15. $10 \cdot 4 = \square$

16. $2\overline{)20}$
17. $70 \div 10 = \square$
18. $9 * \square = 18$

19. $\square \times 5 = 35$
20. $\frac{\square}{3} = 10$
21. $\square \cdot 2 = 16$

1. 20 2. 3 3. 8 4. 8 5. 8 6. 6 7. 6 8. 12 9. 60 10. 5 11. 70 12. 7 13. 18 14. 9 15. 40 16. 10 17. 7 18. 2 19. 7 20. 30 21. 8

4-6 Name _____ Date _____

Homework

Study Plan

Homework Helper

Solve each problem.

1. Wendy has $2.00. She wants to buy some marbles that cost $0.10 each. How many marbles can she buy?

2. Natalie turned off 2 lights in each of the 6 rooms of her house. How many lights did she turn off?

3. Luis has 18 single socks. How many pairs of socks does he have?

4. Lana has 9 nickels. She wants to buy an apple that cost $0.40. Does she have enough money?

5. Annabelle had 20 crayons. She gave 5 of them to each of her sisters. How many sisters does Annabelle have?

6. Harvey wrote letters to 10 of his friends. Each letter was 3 pages long. How many pages did Harvey write?

Complete the table.

7.

Number of Nickels	1	3	5	8	
Total Amount		15¢		45¢	50¢

UNIT 4 LESSON 6 Multiply and Divide with 10 **125**

4-6 Name _____ Date _____

> Vera had 163 marbles. Her older brother gave her his collection of 297 marbles. How many marbles does Vera have now?

1. Solve the problem. _____   *Show your work.*

2. Write a subtraction word problem related to the addition word problem. _____

   _____

   _____

3. Without doing any calculations, find the solution to the problem you wrote. _____

   _____

> Jose spent $6.87 at the store. He spent $3.96 on markers and the rest on crayons. How much money did he spend on crayons?

4. Solve the problem. _____   *Show your work.*

5. Write an addition word problem related to the subtraction word problem.

   _____

   _____

   _____

6. Without doing any calculations, find the solution to the problem you wrote. _____

Use mental math to add or subtract.

7. 800 + 100 = _____   8. 540 − 20 = _____

9. 630 + 300 = _____   10. 300 − 150 = _____

126 UNIT 4 LESSON 6   Multiply and Divide with 10

4-7 Homework

Use this chart to practice your 9s count-bys, multiplications, and divisions. Then have your Homework Helper test you.

	× In Order	× Mixed Up	÷ Mixed Up
9s	1 × 9 = 9	4 × 9 = 36	63 ÷ 9 = 7
	2 × 9 = 18	7 × 9 = 63	9 ÷ 9 = 1
	3 × 9 = 27	2 × 9 = 18	54 ÷ 9 = 6
	4 × 9 = 36	5 × 9 = 45	18 ÷ 9 = 2
	5 × 9 = 45	9 × 9 = 81	90 ÷ 9 = 10
	6 × 9 = 54	1 × 9 = 9	81 ÷ 9 = 9
	7 × 9 = 63	10 × 9 = 90	45 ÷ 9 = 5
	8 × 9 = 72	3 × 9 = 27	27 ÷ 9 = 3
	9 × 9 = 81	6 × 9 = 54	36 ÷ 9 = 4
	10 × 9 = 90	8 × 9 = 72	72 ÷ 9 = 8

4-7 Homework

Name _____ Date _____

Multiply or divide to find the missing numbers. Then check your answers at the bottom of this page.

1. $2 \times 9 = \square$
2. $18 \div 2 = \square$
3. $6 * \square = 12$
4. $40 / 5 = \square$
5. $10 \cdot 8 = \square$
6. $\frac{27}{9} = \square$
7. $\square \times 5 = 40$
8. $2\overline{)14}$ (quotient $\square$)
9. $9 \times 10 = \square$
10. $\frac{60}{10} = \square$
11. $10 \cdot 7 = \square$
12. $72 \div 9 = \square$
13. $2 * 9 = \square$
14. $\frac{20}{2} = \square$
15. $9 \cdot \square = 36$
16. $10 / 2 = \square$
17. $63 \div 9 = \square$
18. $9 * 9 = \square$
19. $5 \times 5 = \square$
20. $5\overline{)30}$ (quotient $\square$)
21. $9 \times 3 = \square$

Answers: 1. 18 2. 9 3. 2 4. 8 5. 80 6. 3 7. 8 8. 7 9. 90 10. 6 11. 70 12. 18 13. 18 14. 10 15. 4 16. 5 17. 7 18. 81 19. 25 20. 6 21. 27

128 UNIT 4 LESSON 7. Multiply and Divide with 9

Home Check Sheet 2: 10s and 9s

10s Multiplications	10s Divisions	9s Multiplications	9s Divisions
9 × 10 = 90	100 / 10 = 10	3 × 9 = 27	27 / 9 = 3
10 • 3 = 30	50 ÷ 10 = 5	9 • 7 = 63	9 ÷ 9 = 1
10 * 6 = 60	70 / 10 = 7	10 * 9 = 90	81 / 9 = 9
1 × 10 = 10	40 ÷ 10 = 4	5 × 9 = 45	45 ÷ 9 = 5
10 • 4 = 40	80 / 10 = 8	9 • 8 = 72	90 / 9 = 10
10 * 7 = 70	60 ÷ 10 = 6	9 * 1 = 9	36 ÷ 9 = 4
8 × 10 = 80	10 / 10 = 1	2 × 9 = 18	18 / 9 = 2
10 • 10 = 100	20 ÷ 10 = 2	9 • 9 = 81	63 ÷ 9 = 7
5 * 10 = 50	90 / 10 = 9	6 * 9 = 54	54 / 9 = 6
10 × 2 = 20	30 / 10 = 3	9 × 4 = 36	72 / 9 = 8
10 • 5 = 50	80 ÷ 10 = 8	9 • 5 = 45	27 ÷ 9 = 3
4 * 10 = 40	70 / 10 = 7	4 * 9 = 36	45 / 9 = 5
10 × 1 = 10	100 ÷ 10 = 10	9 × 1 = 9	63 / 9 = 7
3 • 10 = 30	90 / 10 = 9	3 • 9 = 27	72 / 9 = 8
10 * 8 = 80	60 ÷ 10 = 6	9 * 8 = 72	54 ÷ 9 = 6
7 × 10 = 70	30 / 10 = 3	7 × 9 = 63	18 / 9 = 2
6 • 10 = 60	10 ÷ 10 = 1	6 • 9 = 54	90 ÷ 9 = 10
10 * 9 = 90	40 ÷ 10 = 4	9 * 9 = 81	9 ÷ 9 = 1
10 × 10 = 100	20 / 10 = 2	10 × 9 = 90	36 / 9 = 4
2 • 10 = 20	50 ÷ 10 = 5	2 • 9 = 18	81 ÷ 9 = 9

Home Check Sheet 2: 10s and 9s

4-8 Homework

Home Check Sheet 3: 2s, 5s, 9s, and 10s

2s, 5s, 9s, 10s Multiplications	2s, 5s, 9s, 10s Multiplications	2s, 5s, 9s, 10s Divisions	2s, 5s, 9s, 10s Divisions
2 × 10 = 20	5 × 10 = 50	18 / 2 = 9	36 / 9 = 4
10 • 5 = 50	10 • 9 = 90	50 ÷ 5 = 10	70 ÷ 10 = 7
9 * 6 = 54	4 * 10 = 40	72 / 9 = 8	18 / 2 = 9
7 × 10 = 70	2 × 9 = 18	60 ÷ 10 = 6	45 ÷ 5 = 9
2 • 3 = 6	5 • 3 = 15	12 / 2 = 6	45 / 9 = 5
5 * 7 = 35	6 * 9 = 54	30 ÷ 5 = 6	30 ÷ 10 = 3
9 × 10 = 90	10 × 3 = 30	18 / 9 = 2	6 / 2 = 3
6 • 10 = 60	3 • 2 = 6	50 ÷ 10 = 5	50 ÷ 5 = 10
8 * 2 = 16	5 * 8 = 40	14 / 2 = 7	27 / 9 = 3
5 × 6 = 30	9 × 9 = 81	25 / 5 = 5	70 / 10 = 7
9 • 5 = 45	10 • 4 = 40	81 ÷ 9 = 9	20 ÷ 2 = 10
8 * 10 = 80	9 * 2 = 18	20 / 10 = 2	45 / 5 = 9
2 × 1 = 2	5 × 1 = 5	8 ÷ 2 = 4	54 ÷ 9 = 6
3 • 5 = 15	9 • 6 = 54	45 / 5 = 9	80 / 10 = 8
4 * 9 = 36	10 * 1 = 10	63 ÷ 9 = 7	16 ÷ 2 = 8
3 × 10 = 30	7 × 2 = 14	30 / 10 = 3	15 / 5 = 3
2 • 6 = 12	6 • 5 = 30	10 ÷ 2 = 5	90 ÷ 9 = 10
4 * 5 = 20	8 * 9 = 72	40 ÷ 5 = 8	100 ÷ 10 = 10
9 × 7 = 63	10 × 6 = 60	9 / 9 = 1	12 / 2 = 6
1 • 10 = 10	2 • 8 = 16	50 ÷ 10 = 5	35 ÷ 5 = 7

4-8 Homework

Multiply or divide to find the missing numbers. Then check your answers at the bottom of this page.

1. $5 \times 6 = \square$
2. $50 \div 10 = \square$
3. $6 * 9 = \square$

4. $12 / 2 = \square$
5. $9 \times \square = 72$
6. $\frac{14}{2} = \square$

7. $9 \cdot 5 = \square$
8. $15 \div 5 = \square$
9. $7 \times 2 = \square$

10. $25 / 5 = \square$
11. $10 \cdot \square = 40$
12. $9 \overline{)27}$

13. $8 * 5 = \square$
14. $\frac{81}{9} = \square$
15. $7 \cdot \square = 35$

16. $2 \overline{)20}$
17. $10 \div \square = 5$
18. $2 * 7 = \square$

19. $30 \div 5 = \square$
20. $2 \times 7 = \square$
21. $18 / 2 = \square$

1. 30 2. 5 3. 54 4. 6 5. 8 6. 7 7. 45 8. 3 9. 14 10. 5 11. 4
12. 3 13. 40 14. 9 15. 5 16. 10 17. 2 18. 14 19. 6 20. 14 21. 9

134 UNIT 4 LESSON 8 — Fluency Day for 2s, 5s, 9s, and 10s

4–8 Homework

Study Plan

Homework Helper

Write an equation for each situation. Then solve the problem.

1. Quinn rode his bike 35 miles. He stopped for water every 5 miles. How many times did Quinn stop for water?

   _____

2. Roy had 12 bottles of juice. He put them in the refrigerator in 2 rows. How many bottles were in each row?

   _____

3. Melinda has 5 cousins. She called each one on the phone 4 times this month. How many phone calls did she make to her cousins this month?

   _____

4. Janelle won 27 tickets at the fair. She traded the tickets for 9 prizes. Each prize was worth the same number of tickets. How many tickets were each prize worth?

   _____

5. Eric had 2 picnic baskets. He put 7 apples in each one. How many apples did he put into the picnic baskets?

   _____

6. Grace has read 2 chapters in each of her 9 books. How many chapters has she read in all?

   _____

4-8 Remembering

Solve each problem.

Show your work.

1. Jake had 16 model planes. He gave 4 of them to his brother. How many model planes did Jake have left?

   _____

2. Ahmed and Tray are playing air hockey. Ahmed has made 10 goals. He has made 3 more goals than Tray. How many goals has Tray made?

   _____

3. There are 875 students at Prairie Hill School. Of these students, 467 are in the elementary school. The rest are in junior high. How many students are in junior high?

   _____

Use the bar graph to solve each problem.

4. How much money was earned altogether from the sale of artwork and trips?

   _____

5. How much more money was earned from the sale of artwork than furniture?

   _____

6. Write a problem using the information in the bar graph. Solve your problem.

   _____
   _____

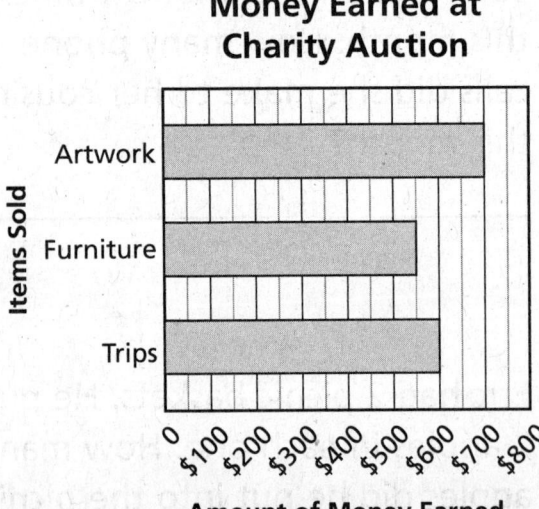

Money Earned at Charity Auction

Fluency Day for 2s, 5s, 9s, and 10s

Homework

4–9

Name _____ Date _____

Use this chart to practice your 3s count-bys, multiplications, and divisions. Then have your Homework Helper test you.

	× In Order	× Mixed Up	Mixed Up
3s	1 × 3 = 3	3 × 3 = 9	27 ÷ 3 = 9
	2 × 3 = 6	5 × 3 = 15	21 ÷ 3 = 7
	3 × 3 = 9	1 × 3 = 3	3 ÷ 3 = 1
	4 × 3 = 12	8 × 3 = 24	9 ÷ 3 = 3
	5 × 3 = 15	2 × 3 = 6	30 ÷ 3 = 10
	6 × 3 = 18	9 × 3 = 27	24 ÷ 3 = 8
	7 × 3 = 21	7 × 3 = 21	12 ÷ 3 = 4
	8 × 3 = 24	10 × 3 = 30	6 ÷ 3 = 2
	9 × 3 = 27	6 × 3 = 18	15 ÷ 3 = 5
	10 × 3 = 30	4 × 3 = 12	18 ÷ 3 = 6

4-9 Homework

Multiply or divide to find the missing numbers. Then check your answers at the bottom of this page.

1. 6 × 3 = ☐
2. 3)2̄7̄ (with ☐ on top)
3. 2 * ☐ = 18

4. 18 / 9 = ☐
5. 3 × ☐ = 30
6. $\frac{15}{3}$ = ☐

7. 9 • 8 = ☐
8. 50 ÷ 10 = ☐
9. 2 × 2 = ☐

10. 35 / 5 = ☐
11. 4 • 10 = ☐
12. 14 ÷ 2 = ☐

13. 8 * 3 = ☐
14. $\frac{63}{9}$ = ☐
15. 5 • ☐ = 35

16. 9)2̄7̄ (with ☐ on top)
17. 10 ÷ ☐ = 2
18. ☐ * 9 = 18

19. 5 × 9 = ☐
20. 81 ÷ ☐ = 9
21. 14 / 2 = ☐

1. 18 2. 9 3. 9 4. 2 5. 10 6. 5 7. 72 8. 5 9. 4 10. 7 11. 40 12. 7 13. 24 14. 7 15. 7 16. 3 17. 5 18. 2 19. 45 20. 9 21. 7

138 UNIT 4 LESSON 9 Multiply and Divide with 3

2×2	2　　3 ×3　×2	2×4 4×2	2　　5 ×5　×2
2×6 6×2	2　　7 ×7　×2	2×8 8×2	2　　9 ×9　×2

10 = 2 × 5	2 4	6 = 2 × 3	2
10 = 5 × 2	×4 ×2	6 = 3 × 2	×2
	8 8		4

18 = 2 × 9	2 8	14 = 2 × 7	2 6
18 = 9 × 2	×8 ×2	14 = 7 × 2	×6 ×2
	16 16		12 12

| 3×3 | 3   4 | 3×5 | 3   6 |
| | ×4 ×3 | 5×3 | ×6   ×3 |

| 3×7 | 3   8 | 3×9 | 4 |
| 7×3 | ×8   ×3 | 9×3 | ×4 |

UNIT 4 LESSON 10   Home Multiplication Strategy Cards

Card 1
18 = 3 × 6
18 = 6 × 3

6	3
12	6
18	9
	12
	15
	18

3 × 6 = 18 array

Card 2
3 × 5 = 15 ; 5 × 3 = 15

5	3
10	6
15	9
	12
	15

5 × 3 = 15 array

Card 3
12 = 3 × 4
12 = 4 × 3

4	3
8	6
12	9
	12

3 × 4 = 12 array

Card 4
3 × 3 = 9

3
6
9

3 × 3 = 9 array

Card 5
16 = 4 × 4

4
8
12
16

4 × 4 = 16 array

Card 6
3 × 9 = 27 ; 9 × 3 = 27

9	3
18	6
27	9
	12
	15
	18
	21
	24
	27

3 × 9 = 27 array

Card 7
24 = 3 × 8
24 = 8 × 3

8	3
16	6
24	9
	12
	15
	18
	21
	24

8 × 3 = 24 array

Card 8
3 × 7 = 21 ; 7 × 3 = 21

7	3
14	6
21	9
	12
	15
	18
	21

3 × 7 = 21 array

Home Multiplication Strategy Cards

| 4 × 5 | 4 | 6 | 4 × 7 | 4 | 8 |
| 5 × 4 | × 6 | × 4 | 7 × 4 | × 8 | × 4 |

| 4 × 9 | 5 | 5 × 6 | 5 | 7 |
| 9 × 4 | × 5 | 6 × 5 | × 7 | × 5 |

UNIT 4 LESSON 10   Home Multiplication Strategy Cards **145**

Card 1

32 = 4 × 8
32 = 8 × 4

8	4
16	8
24	12
32	16
	20
	24
	28
	32

4
8 × 32

Card 2

  4   7
× 7   × 4
 28   28

7	4
14	8
21	12
28	16
	20
	24
	28

7
4 × 28

Card 3

24 = 4 × 6
24 = 6 × 4

6	4
12	8
18	12
24	16
	20
	24

4
6 × 24

Card 4

  4   5
× 5   × 4
 20   20

5	4
10	8
15	12
20	16
	20

5
4 × 20

Card 5

35 = 5 × 7
35 = 7 × 5

7	5
14	10
21	15
28	20
35	25
	30
	35

7
5 × 35

Card 6

  5   6
× 6   × 5
 30   30

6	5
12	10
18	15
24	20
30	25
	30

5
6 × 30

Card 7

25 = 5 × 5

5
10
15
20
25

5
5 × 25

Card 8

  4   9
× 9   × 4
 36   36

9	4
18	8
27	12
36	16
	20
	24
	28
	32
	36

9
4 × 36

146 UNIT 4 LESSON 10

Home Multiplication Strategy Cards

| 5 × 8 | 5 | 9 | 6 × 6 | 6 | 7 |
| 8 × 5 | × 9 | × 5 | | × 7 | × 6 |

| 6 × 8 | 6 | 9 | 7 × 7 | 7 | 8 |
| 8 × 6 | × 9 | × 6 | | × 8 | × 7 |

UNIT 4 LESSON 10

Home Multiplication Strategy Cards **147**

Card 1
42 = 7 × 6
42 = 6 × 7

6	7
12	14
18	21
24	28
30	35
36	42
42	

7 × 6 = 42

Card 2
6
× 6

36

6
12
18
24
30
36

6 × 6 = 36

Card 3
45 = 9 × 5
45 = 5 × 9

5	9
10	18
15	27
20	36
25	45
30	
35	
40	
45	

9 × 5 = 45

Card 4
8   5
× 5   × 8
---   ---
40   40

5	8
10	16
15	24
20	32
25	40
30	
35	
40	

5 × 8 = 40

Card 5
56 = 7 × 8
56 = 8 × 7

8	7
16	14
24	21
32	28
40	35
48	42
56	49
	56

8 × 7 = 56

Card 6
7
× 7

49

7
14
21
28
35
42
49

7 × 7 = 49

Card 7
54 = 9 × 6
54 = 6 × 9

6	9
12	18
18	27
24	36
30	45
36	54
42	
48	
54	

9 × 6 = 54

Card 8
6   8
× 8   × 6
---   ---
48   48

6	8
12	16
18	24
24	32
30	40
36	48
42	
48	

8 × 6 = 48

Home Multiplication Strategy Cards

| 7 × 9 | 8 | 9 × 8 | 9 |
| 9 × 7 | × 8 | 8 × 9 | × 9 |

UNIT 4 LESSON 10

Card 1

81 = 9 × 9

9
18
27
36
45

54
63
72
81

9
9 | 81

Card 2

```
  9        8
× 8      × 9
---     ----
 72       72
```

8   9
16   18
24   27
32   36
40   45

48   54
56   63
64   72
72

9
8 | 72

Card 3

64 = 8 × 8

8
16
24
32
40

48
56
64

8
8 | 64

Card 4

```
  7        9
× 9      × 7
---      ---
 63       63
```

9   7
18   14
27   21
36   28
45   35

54   42
63   49
     56
     63

9
7 | 63

2)4̄	2)6̄	2)8̄	2)1̄0̄
4 ÷ 2	6 ÷ 2	8 ÷ 2	10 ÷ 2

2)1̄2̄	2)1̄4̄	2)1̄6̄	2)1̄8̄
12 ÷ 2	14 ÷ 2	16 ÷ 2	18 ÷ 2

Home Division Strategy Cards

Card 1
```
    5           2
2)10        5)10
2           5
4          10
6
8
10
```
2 • • • • • 5
  • 10

Card 2
```
    4           2
2)8         4)8
2           4
4           8
6
8
```
2 • • • • 4
  • 8

Card 3
```
    3           2
2)6         3)6
2           3
4           6
6
```
2 • • • 3
  • 6

Card 4
```
    2
2)4
2
4
```
2 • • 2
  • 4

Card 5
```
    9           2
2)18        9)18
2           9
4          18
6
8
10
12
14
16
18
```
2 • • • • • • • • • 9
  • 18

Card 6
```
    8           2
2)16        8)16
2           8
4          16
6
8
10
12
14
16
```
2 • • • • • • • • 8
  • 16

Card 7
```
    7           2
2)14        7)14
2           7
4          14
6
8
10
12
14
```
2 • • • • • • • 7
  • 14

Card 8
```
    6           2
2)12        6)12
2           6
4          12
6
8
10
12
```
2 • • • • • • 6
  • 12

152 UNIT 4 LESSON 10

$3\overline{)6}$	$4\overline{)8}$	$5\overline{)10}$	$6\overline{)12}$
$6 \div 3$	$8 \div 4$	$10 \div 5$	$12 \div 6$

$7\overline{)14}$	$8\overline{)16}$	$9\overline{)18}$	$3\overline{)9}$
$14 \div 7$	$16 \div 8$	$18 \div 9$	$9 \div 3$

$\overset{2}{\overline{)12}}$ $\overset{6}{\overline{)12}}$
6)12 2)12
6   2
12 4
    6
    8
    10
    12
	$\overset{2}{\overline{)10}}$ $\overset{5}{\overline{)10}}$
	5)10 2)10
	5 2
	10 4
	    6
	    8
	    10

Home Division Strategy Cards

154 UNIT 4 LESSON 10

$3\overline{)12}$	$3\overline{)15}$	$3\overline{)18}$	$3\overline{)21}$
$12 \div 3$	$15 \div 3$	$18 \div 3$	$21 \div 3$

$3\overline{)24}$	$3\overline{)27}$	$4\overline{)12}$	$5\overline{)15}$
$24 \div 3$	$27 \div 3$	$12 \div 4$	$15 \div 5$

Card 1

```
   7           3
3)21        7)21
 3            7
 6           14
 9           21
12
15
18
21
```

         7
    o o o o o o o
3 o   21
    o

Card 2

```
   6           3
3)18        6)18
 3            6
 6           12
 9           18
12
15
18
```

         6
    o o o o o o
3 o   18
    o

Card 3

```
   5           3
3)15        5)15
 3            5
 6           10
 9           15
12
15
```

         5
    o o o o o
3 o   15
    o

Card 4

```
   4           3
3)12        4)12
 3            4
 6            8
 9           12
12
```

         4
    o o o o
3 o   12
    o

Card 5

```
   3           5
5)15        3)15
 5            3
10            6
15            9
             12
             15
```

         3
    o o o
5 o
  o 15
  o
  o

Card 6

```
   3           4
4)12        3)12
 4            3
 8            6
12            9
             12
```

         3
    o o o
4 o 12
  o
  o

Card 7

```
   9           3
3)27        9)27
 3            9
 6           18
 9           27
12
15
18
21
24
27
```

         9
    o o o o o o o o o
3 o   27
    o

Card 8

```
   8           3
3)24        8)24
 3            8
 6           16
 9           24
12
15
18
21
24
```

         8
    o o o o o o o o
3 o   24
    o

156 UNIT 4 LESSON 10

$6\overline{)18}$	$7\overline{)21}$	$8\overline{)24}$	$9\overline{)27}$
$18 \div 6$	$21 \div 7$	$24 \div 8$	$27 \div 9$

$4\overline{)16}$	$4\overline{)20}$	$4\overline{)24}$	$4\overline{)28}$
$16 \div 4$	$20 \div 4$	$24 \div 4$	$28 \div 4$

Home Division Strategy Cards

Card 1
3 | 9
9)27 | 3)27
9 | 3
18 | 6
27 | 9
| 12
| 15
| 18
| 21
| 24
| 27

3
9 • 27

Card 2
3 | 8
8)24 | 3)24
8 | 3
16 | 6
24 | 9
| 12
| 15
| 18
| 21
| 24

3
8 • 24

Card 3
3 | 7
7)21 | 3)21
7 | 3
14 | 6
21 | 9
| 12
| 15
| 18
| 21

3
7 • 21

Card 4
3 | 6
6)18 | 3)18
6 | 3
12 | 6
18 | 9
| 12
| 15
| 18

3
6 • 18

Card 5
7 | 4
4)28 | 7)28
4 | 7
8 | 14
12 | 21
16 | 28
20
24
28

7
4 • 28

Card 6
6 | 4
4)24 | 6)24
4 | 6
8 | 12
12 | 18
16 | 24
20
24

6
4 • 24

Card 7
5 | 4
4)20 | 5)20
4 | 5
8 | 10
12 | 15
16 | 20
20

5
4 • 20

Card 8
4
4)16
4
8
12
16

4
4 • 16

158 UNIT 4 LESSON 10

$4\overline{)32}$	$4\overline{)36}$	$5\overline{)20}$	$6\overline{)24}$
$32 \div 4$	$36 \div 4$	$20 \div 5$	$24 \div 6$

$7\overline{)28}$	$8\overline{)32}$	$9\overline{)36}$	$5\overline{)25}$
$28 \div 7$	$32 \div 8$	$36 \div 9$	$25 \div 5$

Card 1

$6\overline{)24}$ $4\overline{)24}$
 6   4
12   8
18   12
24   16
     20
     24

Card 2

$5\overline{)20}$ $4\overline{)20}$
 5   4
10   8
15   12
20   16
     20

Card 3

$4\overline{)36}$ $9\overline{)36}$
 4   9
 8   18
12   27
16   36
20
24
28
32
36

Card 4

$4\overline{)32}$ $8\overline{)32}$
 4   8
 8   16
12   24
16   32
20
24
28
32

Card 5

$5\overline{)25}$
 5
10
15
20
25

Card 6

$9\overline{)36}$ $4\overline{)36}$
 9   4
18   8
27   12
36   16
     20
     24
     28
     32
     36

Card 7

$8\overline{)32}$ $4\overline{)32}$
 8   4
16   8
24   12
32   16
     20
     24
     28
     32

Card 8

$7\overline{)28}$ $4\overline{)28}$
 7   4
14   8
21   12
28   16
     20
     24
     28

160 UNIT 4 LESSON 10

Home Division Strategy Cards

5)30	5)35	5)40	5)45
30 ÷ 5	35 ÷ 5	40 ÷ 5	45 ÷ 5

6)30	7)35	8)40	9)45
30 ÷ 6	35 ÷ 7	40 ÷ 8	45 ÷ 9

Home Division Strategy Cards

Card 1
```
    9         5
 5)45      9)45
  5          9
 10         18
 15         27
 20         36
 25         45
 30
 35
 40
 45
```
9 across, 5 down, 45

Card 2
```
    8         5
 5)40      8)40
  5          8
 10         16
 15         24
 20         32
 25         40
 30
 35
 40
```
8 across, 5 down, 40

Card 3
```
    7         5
 5)35      7)35
  5          7
 10         14
 15         21
 20         28
 25         35
 30
 35
```
7 across, 5 down, 35

Card 4
```
    6         5
 5)30      6)30
  5          6
 10         12
 15         18
 20         24
 25         30
 30
```
6 across, 5 down, 30

Card 5
```
    5         9
 9)45      5)45
  9          5
 18         10
 27         15
 36         20
 45         25
             30
             35
             40
             45
```
5 across, 9 down, 45

Card 6
```
    5         8
 8)40      5)40
  8          5
 16         10
 24         15
 32         20
 40         25
             30
             35
             40
```
5 across, 8 down, 40

Card 7
```
    5         7
 7)35      5)35
  7          5
 14         10
 21         15
 28         20
 35         25
             30
             35
```
5 across, 7 down, 35

Card 8
```
    5         6
 6)30      5)30
  6          5
 12         10
 18         15
 24         20
 30         25
             30
```
5 across, 6 down, 30

$6\overline{)36}$	$6\overline{)42}$	$6\overline{)48}$	$6\overline{)54}$
$36 \div 6$	$42 \div 6$	$48 \div 6$	$54 \div 6$

$7\overline{)42}$	$8\overline{)48}$	$9\overline{)54}$	$7\overline{)49}$
$42 \div 7$	$48 \div 8$	$54 \div 9$	$49 \div 7$

Card 1

$$6\overline{)54}\quad 9\overline{)54}$$

9	6
6	9
12	18
18	27
24	36
30	45
36	54
42	
48	
54	

9 across, 6 down, 54

Card 2

$$6\overline{)48}\quad 8\overline{)48}$$

8	6
6	8
12	16
18	24
24	32
30	40
36	48
42	
48	

8 across, 6 down, 48

Card 3

$$6\overline{)42}\quad 7\overline{)42}$$

7	6
6	7
12	14
18	21
24	28
30	35
36	42
42	

7 across, 6 down, 42

Card 4

$$6\overline{)36}$$

6
6
12
18
24
30
36

6 across, 6 down, 36

Card 5

$$7\overline{)49}$$

7
7
14
21
28
35
42
49

7 across, 7 down, 49

Card 6

$$9\overline{)54}\quad 6\overline{)54}$$

6	9
9	6
18	12
27	18
36	24
45	30
54	36
	42
	48
	54

6 across, 9 down, 54

Card 7

$$8\overline{)48}\quad 6\overline{)48}$$

6	8
8	6
16	12
24	18
32	24
40	30
48	36
	42
	48

6 across, 8 down, 48

Card 8

$$7\overline{)42}\quad 6\overline{)42}$$

6	7
7	6
14	12
21	18
28	24
35	30
42	36
	42

6 across, 7 down, 42

164 UNIT 4 LESSON 10

Home Division Strategy Cards

7)56	7)63	8)56	9)63
56 ÷ 7	63 ÷ 7	56 ÷ 8	63 ÷ 9

8)64	8)72	9)72	9)81
64 ÷ 8	72 ÷ 8	72 ÷ 9	81 ÷ 9

Home Division Strategy Cards

Card 1

$$7 \\ 9\overline{)63} \quad 7\overline{)63} \\ 9$$

9	7
18	14
27	21
36	28
45	35
54	42
63	49
	56
	63

7 across top, 9 down side, 63 inside

Card 2

$$7 \\ 8\overline{)56} \quad 7\overline{)56} \\ 8$$

8	7
16	14
24	21
32	28
40	35
48	42
56	49
	56

7 across top, 8 down side, 56 inside

Card 3

$$9 \\ 7\overline{)63} \quad 9\overline{)63} \\ 7$$

7	9
14	18
21	27
28	36
35	45
42	54
49	63
56	
63	

9 across top, 7 down side, 63 inside

Card 4

$$8 \\ 7\overline{)56} \quad 8\overline{)56} \\ 7$$

7	8
14	16
21	24
28	32
35	40
42	48
49	56
56	

8 across top, 7 down side, 56 inside

Card 5

$$9 \\ 9\overline{)81}$$

9
18
27
36
45
54
63
72
81

9 across top, 9 down side, 81 inside

Card 6

$$8 \\ 9\overline{)72} \quad 8\overline{)72} \\ 9$$

9	8
18	16
27	24
36	32
45	40
54	48
63	56
72	64
	72

8 across top, 9 down side, 72 inside

Card 7

$$9 \\ 8\overline{)72} \quad 9\overline{)72} \\ 8$$

8	9
16	18
24	27
32	36
40	45
48	54
56	63
64	72
72	

9 across top, 8 down side, 72 inside

Card 8

$$8 \\ 8\overline{)64}$$

8
16
24
32
40
48
56
64

8 across top, 8 down side, 64 inside

Home Division Strategy Cards

4–10 Homework

Home Study Sheet B

3s

Count-bys	Mixed Up ×	Mixed Up ÷
1 × 3 = 3	5 × 3 = 15	27 ÷ 3 = 9
2 × 3 = 6	1 × 3 = 3	6 ÷ 3 = 2
3 × 3 = 9	8 × 3 = 24	18 ÷ 3 = 6
4 × 3 = 12	10 × 3 = 30	30 ÷ 3 = 10
5 × 3 = 15	3 × 3 = 9	9 ÷ 3 = 3
6 × 3 = 18	7 × 3 = 21	3 ÷ 3 = 1
7 × 3 = 21	9 × 3 = 27	12 ÷ 3 = 4
8 × 3 = 24	2 × 3 = 6	24 ÷ 3 = 8
9 × 3 = 27	4 × 3 = 12	15 ÷ 3 = 5
10 × 3 = 30	6 × 3 = 18	21 ÷ 3 = 7

4s

Count-bys	Mixed Up ×	Mixed Up ÷
1 × 4 = 4	4 × 4 = 16	12 ÷ 4 = 3
2 × 4 = 8	1 × 4 = 4	36 ÷ 4 = 9
3 × 4 = 12	7 × 4 = 28	24 ÷ 4 = 6
4 × 4 = 16	3 × 4 = 12	4 ÷ 4 = 1
5 × 4 = 20	9 × 4 = 36	20 ÷ 4 = 5
6 × 4 = 24	10 × 4 = 40	28 ÷ 4 = 7
7 × 4 = 28	2 × 4 = 8	8 ÷ 4 = 2
8 × 4 = 32	5 × 4 = 20	40 ÷ 4 = 10
9 × 4 = 36	8 × 4 = 32	32 ÷ 4 = 8
10 × 4 = 40	6 × 4 = 24	16 ÷ 4 = 4

0s

Count-bys	Mixed Up ×
1 × 0 = 0	3 × 0 = 0
2 × 0 = 0	10 × 0 = 0
3 × 0 = 0	5 × 0 = 0
4 × 0 = 0	8 × 0 = 0
5 × 0 = 0	7 × 0 = 0
6 × 0 = 0	2 × 0 = 0
7 × 0 = 0	9 × 0 = 0
8 × 0 = 0	6 × 0 = 0
9 × 0 = 0	1 × 0 = 0
10 × 0 = 0	4 × 0 = 0

1s

Count-bys	Mixed Up ×	Mixed Up ÷
1 × 1 = 1	5 × 1 = 5	10 ÷ 1 = 10
2 × 1 = 2	7 × 1 = 7	8 ÷ 1 = 8
3 × 1 = 3	10 × 1 = 10	4 ÷ 1 = 4
4 × 1 = 4	1 × 1 = 1	9 ÷ 1 = 9
5 × 1 = 5	8 × 1 = 8	6 ÷ 1 = 6
6 × 1 = 6	4 × 1 = 4	7 ÷ 1 = 7
7 × 1 = 7	9 × 1 = 9	1 ÷ 1 = 1
8 × 1 = 8	3 × 1 = 3	2 ÷ 1 = 2
9 × 1 = 9	2 × 1 = 2	5 ÷ 1 = 5
10 × 1 = 10	6 × 1 = 6	3 ÷ 1 = 3

4–10 Homework

Multiply or divide to find the missing numbers. Then check your answers at the bottom of the page.

1. $3 \times 5 = \boxed{}$
2. $27 \div 9 = \boxed{}$
3. $2\overline{)20}$

4. $7 \cdot 9 = \boxed{}$
5. $2 * \boxed{} = 12$
6. $18 / 3 = \boxed{}$

7. $9 \times 5 = \boxed{}$
8. $3 * \boxed{} = 21$
9. $\frac{81}{9} = \boxed{}$

10. $6 \div 3 = \boxed{}$
11. $8 \times 2 = \boxed{}$
12. $\frac{14}{2} = \boxed{}$

13. $3 \cdot 3 = \boxed{}$
14. $\boxed{} * 9 = 72$
15. $90 \div 9 = \boxed{}$

16. $\boxed{} * 2 = 18$
17. $24 \div \boxed{} = 8$
18. $12 / \boxed{} = 6$

19. $6 \cdot 5 = \boxed{}$
20. $4 \times \boxed{} = 40$
21. $\boxed{} \cdot 9 = 54$

1. 15 2. 3 3. 10 4. 63 5. 6 6. 6 7. 45 8. 7 9. 9 10. 2 11. 16 12. 7 13. 9 14. 8 15. 10 16. 9 17. 3 18. 2 19. 30 20. 10 21. 6

Multiplication and Area

4-12 Homework

Use this table to practice your 4s Count-bys, multiplications, and divisions. Then have your homework helper test you.

4s	× In Order	× Mixed Up	÷ Mixed Up
	1 × 4 = 4	9 × 4 = 36	20 ÷ 4 = 5
	2 × 4 = 8	5 × 4 = 20	4 ÷ 4 = 1
	3 × 4 = 12	7 × 4 = 28	16 ÷ 4 = 4
	4 × 4 = 16	2 × 4 = 8	36 ÷ 4 = 9
	5 × 4 = 20	4 × 4 = 16	24 ÷ 4 = 6
	6 × 4 = 24	1 × 4 = 4	12 ÷ 4 = 3
	7 × 4 = 28	6 × 4 = 24	32 ÷ 4 = 8
	8 × 4 = 32	8 × 4 = 32	8 ÷ 4 = 2
	9 × 4 = 36	3 × 4 = 12	40 ÷ 4 = 10
	10 × 4 = 40	10 × 4 = 40	28 ÷ 4 = 7

UNIT 4 LESSON 12

4-12

Homework

Multiply or divide to find the missing numbers. Then check your answers at the bottom of this page.

1. $4 \times 9 = \square$

2. $12 \div 3 = \square$

3. $4 * 8 = \square$

4. $30 / 3 = \square$

5. $3 \cdot \square = 24$

6. $9\overline{)81}$ (quotient in box)

7. $6 \times 3 = \square$

8. $\frac{27}{3} = \square$

9. $9 \times 10 = \square$

10. $24 / 4 = \square$

11. $10 \cdot 3 = \square$

12. $16 \div 4 = \square$

13. $9 * \square = 63$

14. $\frac{36}{4} = \square$

15. $7 \cdot 4 = \square$

16. $20 / 4 = \square$

17. $9\overline{)54}$ (quotient in box)

18. $3 * 7 = \square$

19. $\square \times 4 = 4$

20. $15 \div 3 = \square$

21. $4 \times \square = 16$

Answers (upside down at bottom):
1. 36 2. 4 3. 32 4. 10 5. 8 6. 9 7. 18 8. 9 9. 90 10. 6 11. 30
12. 4 13. 7 14. 9 15. 28 16. 5 17. 6 18. 21 19. 1 20. 5 21. 4

174 UNIT 4 LESSON 12   Multiply and Divide with 4

4-12 Homework

Home Check Sheet 4: 3s and 4s

3s Multiplications	3s Divisions	4s Multiplications	4s Divisions
8 × 3 = 24	9 / 3 = 3	1 × 4 = 4	40 / 4 = 10
3 • 2 = 6	21 ÷ 3 = 7	4 • 5 = 20	12 ÷ 4 = 3
3 * 5 = 15	27 / 3 = 9	8 * 4 = 32	24 / 4 = 6
10 × 3 = 30	3 ÷ 3 = 1	3 × 4 = 12	8 ÷ 4 = 2
3 • 3 = 9	18 / 3 = 6	4 • 6 = 24	4 / 4 = 1
3 * 6 = 18	12 ÷ 3 = 4	4 * 9 = 36	28 ÷ 4 = 7
7 × 3 = 21	30 / 3 = 10	10 × 4 = 40	32 / 4 = 8
3 • 9 = 27	6 ÷ 3 = 2	4 • 7 = 28	16 ÷ 4 = 4
4 * 3 = 12	24 / 3 = 8	4 * 4 = 16	36 / 4 = 9
3 × 1 = 3	15 / 3 = 5	2 × 4 = 8	20 / 4 = 5
3 • 4 = 12	21 ÷ 3 = 7	4 • 3 = 12	4 ÷ 4 = 1
3 * 3 = 9	3 / 3 = 1	4 * 2 = 8	32 / 4 = 8
3 × 10 = 30	9 ÷ 3 = 3	9 × 4 = 36	8 ÷ 4 = 2
2 • 3 = 6	27 / 3 = 9	1 • 4 = 4	16 / 4 = 4
3 * 7 = 21	30 ÷ 3 = 10	4 * 6 = 24	36 ÷ 4 = 9
6 × 3 = 18	18 / 3 = 6	5 × 4 = 20	12 / 4 = 3
5 • 3 = 15	6 ÷ 3 = 2	4 • 4 = 16	40 ÷ 4 = 10
3 * 8 = 24	15 ÷ 3 = 5	7 * 4 = 28	20 ÷ 4 = 5
9 × 3 = 27	12 / 3 = 4	8 × 4 = 32	24 / 4 = 6
2 • 3 = 6	24 ÷ 3 = 8	10 • 4 = 40	28 ÷ 4 = 7

4-13 Homework

Study Plan

Homework Helper

Solve.

1. Pablo hung his watercolor paintings in an array with 3 rows and 4 columns. How many paintings did Pablo hang?

   _____

2. A group of 7 friends went on a hiking trip. Each person took 3 granola bars. What total number of granola bars did the friends take?

   _____

3. Jon had 45 sheets of construction paper. He used 9 sheets to make paper snowflakes. How many sheets does he have now?

   _____

You can combine multiplications you know to find multiplications you don't know.

4. Find this product: 5 × 8 = _____

5. Find this product: 1 × 8 = _____

6. Use the answers to numbers 4 and 5 to find this product: 6 × 8 = _____

4-13 Remembering

Use mental math to subtract.

1. 130 − 60 = _____
2. 1,100 − 700 = _____
3. 150 − 90 = _____
4. 1,600 − 800 = _____
5. 120 − 80 = _____
6. 1,300 − 400 = _____

Write a multiplication equation to represent the area of each rectangle.

7.
_____

8.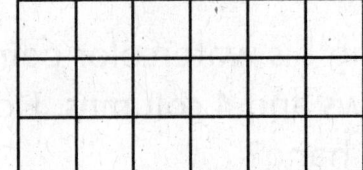
_____

9.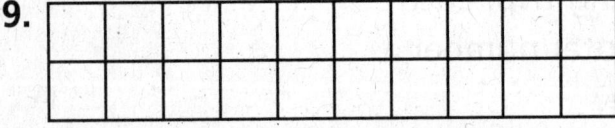
_____

10.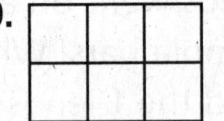
_____

Solve.

11. Mai went to the movies 9 times this month. She paid 4 dollars to see each movie. How much did she spend at the movies?

_____

12. Tess had 45 tomato seeds to plant in her garden. She planted them in an array with 9 rows. How many seeds were in each row?

_____

180 UNIT 4 LESSON 13   Use the Strategy Cards

4-14 Homework

1s

× In Order	× Mixed Up	÷ Mixed Up
1 × 1 = 1	3 × 1 = 3	7 ÷ 1 = 7
2 × 1 = 2	7 × 1 = 7	10 ÷ 1 = 10
3 × 1 = 3	1 × 1 = 1	3 ÷ 1 = 3
4 × 1 = 4	10 × 1 = 10	9 ÷ 1 = 9
5 × 1 = 5	6 × 1 = 6	1 ÷ 1 = 1
6 × 1 = 6	2 × 1 = 2	4 ÷ 1 = 4
7 × 1 = 7	5 × 1 = 5	5 ÷ 1 = 5
8 × 1 = 8	8 × 1 = 8	8 ÷ 1 = 8
9 × 1 = 9	4 × 1 = 4	2 ÷ 1 = 2
10 × 1 = 10	9 × 1 = 9	6 ÷ 1 = 6

0s

× In Order	× Mixed Up
1 × 0 = 0	3 × 0 = 0
2 × 0 = 0	7 × 0 = 0
3 × 0 = 0	1 × 0 = 0
4 × 0 = 0	10 × 0 = 0
5 × 0 = 0	6 × 0 = 0
6 × 0 = 0	2 × 0 = 0
7 × 0 = 0	5 × 0 = 0
8 × 0 = 0	8 × 0 = 0
9 × 0 = 0	4 × 0 = 0
10 × 0 = 0	9 × 0 = 0

4-14 Homework

Find the missing numbers. Then check your answers at the bottom of this page.

1. $4 \times 1 = \square$
2. $12 \div 3 = \square$
3. $7 * 0 = \square$

4. $0 / 5 = \square$
5. $4 \bullet \square = 8$
6. $\frac{2}{1} = \square$

7. $10 \times 1 = \square$
8. $\frac{0}{4} = \square$
9. $1 \times 0 = \square$

10. $3\overline{)9}$ with $\square$ on top
11. $10 \bullet 9 = \square$
12. $0 \div 1 = \square$

13. $3 * \square = 3$
14. $\frac{8}{1} = \square$
15. $0 \bullet 7 = \square$

16. $24 / 3 = \square$
17. $1 \div 1 = \square$
18. $10 * 2 = \square$

19. $\square \times 3 = 0$
20. $3\overline{)18}$ with $\square$ on top
21. $1 \times \square = 4$

22. $\square \times 5 = 25$
23. $6 \bullet 9 = \square$
24. $10 \div 1 = \square$

Answers (upside down at bottom): 1. 4 2. 4 3. 0 4. 0 5. 2 6. 2 7. 10 8. 0 9. 0 10. 3 11. 90 12. 0 13. 1 14. 8 15. 0 16. 8 17. 1 18. 20 19. 0 20. 6 21. 4 22. 5 23. 54 24. 10

Home Check Sheet 5: 1s and 0s

1s Multiplications	1s Divisions	0s Multiplications
1 × 4 = 4	10 / 1 = 10	4 × 0 = 0
5 • 1 = 5	5 ÷ 1 = 5	2 • 0 = 0
7 * 1 = 7	7 / 1 = 7	0 * 8 = 0
1 × 8 = 8	9 ÷ 1 = 9	0 × 5 = 0
1 • 6 = 6	3 / 1 = 3	6 • 0 = 0
10 * 1 = 10	10 ÷ 1 = 10	0 * 7 = 0
1 × 9 = 9	2 / 1 = 2	0 × 2 = 0
3 • 1 = 3	8 ÷ 1 = 8	0 • 9 = 0
1 * 2 = 2	6 / 1 = 6	10 * 0 = 0
1 × 1 = 1	9 / 1 = 9	1 × 0 = 0
8 • 1 = 8	1 ÷ 1 = 1	0 • 6 = 0
1 * 7 = 7	5 / 1 = 5	9 * 0 = 0
1 × 5 = 5	3 ÷ 1 = 3	0 × 4 = 0
6 • 1 = 6	4 / 1 = 4	3 • 0 = 0
1 * 1 = 1	2 ÷ 1 = 2	0 * 3 = 0
1 × 10 = 10	8 / 1 = 8	8 × 0 = 0
9 • 1 = 9	4 ÷ 1 = 4	0 • 10 = 0
4 * 1 = 4	7 ÷ 1 = 7	0 * 1 = 0
2 × 1 = 2	1 / 1 = 1	5 × 0 = 0
1 • 3 = 3	6 ÷ 1 = 6	7 • 0 = 0

Name _____ Date _____

Home Check Sheet 6: Mixed 3s, 4s, 0s, and 1s

3s, 4s, 0s, 1s Multiplications	3s, 4s, 0s, 1s Multiplications	3s, 4s, 1s Divisions	3s, 4s, 1s Divisions
5 × 3 = 15	0 × 5 = 0	18 / 3 = 6	4 / 1 = 4
6 • 4 = 24	10 • 1 = 10	20 ÷ 4 = 5	21 ÷ 3 = 7
9 * 0 = 0	6 * 3 = 18	1 / 1 = 1	16 / 4 = 4
7 × 1 = 7	2 × 4 = 8	21 ÷ 3 = 7	9 ÷ 1 = 9
3 • 3 = 9	5 • 0 = 0	12 / 4 = 3	15 / 3 = 5
4 * 7 = 28	1 * 2 = 2	5 ÷ 1 = 5	8 ÷ 4 = 2
0 × 10 = 0	10 × 3 = 30	15 / 3 = 5	5 / 1 = 5
1 • 6 = 6	5 • 4 = 20	24 ÷ 4 = 6	30 ÷ 3 = 10
3 * 4 = 12	0 * 8 = 0	7 / 1 = 7	12 / 4 = 3
5 × 4 = 20	9 × 2 = 18	12 / 3 = 4	8 / 1 = 8
0 • 5 = 0	10 • 3 = 30	36 ÷ 4 = 9	27 ÷ 3 = 9
9 * 1 = 9	9 * 4 = 36	6 / 1 = 6	40 / 4 = 10
2 × 3 = 6	1 × 0 = 0	12 ÷ 3 = 4	4 ÷ 1 = 4
3 • 4 = 12	1 • 6 = 6	16 / 4 = 4	9 / 3 = 3
0 * 9 = 0	3 * 6 = 18	7 ÷ 1 = 7	16 ÷ 4 = 4
1 × 5 = 5	7 × 4 = 28	9 / 3 = 3	10 / 1 = 10
2 • 3 = 6	6 • 0 = 0	8 ÷ 4 = 2	9 ÷ 3 = 3
4 * 4 = 16	8 * 1 = 8	2 ÷ 1 = 2	20 ÷ 4 = 5
9 × 0 = 0	3 × 9 = 27	6 / 3 = 2	6 / 1 = 6
1 • 1 = 1	1 • 4 = 4	32 ÷ 4 = 8	24 ÷ 3 = 8

4-15

Name _____ **Date** _____

Homework

Study Plan

Homework Helper
_____

Solve each problem.   *Show your work.*

1. Wendy gave 54 apples to her neighbors. She gave away a total of 6 bags of apples. How many apples were in each bag?

   _____

2. Dillon had a box of 45 toy trucks. He gave the trucks to his brother but kept 9 trucks for himself. How many trucks did Dillon give to his brother?

   _____

3. Melissa put 18 stickers in her new sticker album. She put them in 6 rows. How many stickers did she put in each row?

   _____

4. Yan took photographs at the zoo. He took 5 photos in each of the 6 animal houses. How many photos did he take?

   _____

5. Janie stacked some books at the library. She stacked 8 books in 7 different piles. How many books were in the piles?

   _____

UNIT 4 LESSON 15   Play Multiplication and Division Games **187**

4–15 Remembering

Use mental math to find the answer.

1. 40 + 80 − 20 = ___
2. 150 − 70 + 30 = ___
3. 80 + 80 − 30 = ___

4. 70 + 40 − 50 = ___
5. 130 − 50 + 70 = ___
6. 170 − 90 − 30 = ___

Solve each problem.

7. Ants have 6 legs. How many legs are on 8 ants? Find the total by starting with the fifth count-by and counting up from there.

   _____

   ____ ____ ____ ____

8. How many roses are in these 6 vases? Find the total by starting with the fifth count-by and counting up from there.

   _____

   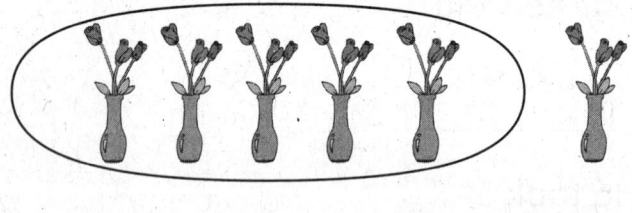

   ____ ____

This Equal-Shares Drawing shows that 6 groups of 4 is the same as 4 groups of 4 plus 2 groups of 4.

9. Find 4 × ④ and 2 × ④ and add the answers.

   _____

10. Find 6 × ④. Did you get the same answer as in number 9?

    _____

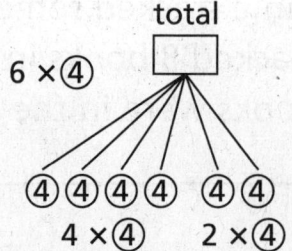

Home Check Sheet 7: 0s, 1s, 2s, 3s, 4s, 5s, 9s, and 10s

0s, 1s, 2s, 3s, 4s, 5s, 9s, 10s Multiplications	0s, 1s, 2s, 3s, 4s, 5s, 9s, 10s Multiplications	1s, 2s, 3s, 4s, 5s, 9s, 10s Divisions	1s, 2s, 3s, 4s, 5s, 9s, 10s Divisions
3 × 0 = 0	0 × 4 = 0	9 / 1 = 9	40 / 10 = 4
7 • 1 = 7	5 • 1 = 5	4 ÷ 2 = 2	7 ÷ 1 = 7
2 * 2 = 4	6 * 7 = 42	9 / 3 = 3	16 / 2 = 8
1 × 3 = 3	2 × 3 = 6	20 ÷ 4 = 5	18 ÷ 3 = 6
4 • 4 = 16	5 • 0 = 0	15 / 5 = 3	16 / 4 = 4
6 * 5 = 30	1 * 1 = 1	45 ÷ 9 = 5	50 ÷ 5 = 10
5 × 9 = 45	10 × 2 = 20	50 / 10 = 5	81 / 9 = 9
0 • 10 = 0	5 • 3 = 15	10 ÷ 1 = 10	30 ÷ 10 = 3
0 * 4 = 0	4 * 5 = 20	8 / 2 = 4	10 / 1 = 10
1 × 8 = 8	5 × 6 = 30	12 / 3 = 4	8 / 2 = 4
2 • 5 = 10	9 • 7 = 63	16 ÷ 4 = 4	27 ÷ 3 = 9
3 * 2 = 6	4 * 10 = 40	35 / 5 = 7	36 / 4 = 9
4 × 3 = 12	6 × 0 = 0	27 ÷ 9 = 3	30 ÷ 5 = 6
5 • 4 = 20	1 • 6 = 6	60 / 10 = 6	9 / 9 = 1
9 * 6 = 54	3 * 2 = 6	7 ÷ 1 = 7	80 ÷ 10 = 8
10 × 7 = 70	7 × 3 = 21	8 / 2 = 4	10 / 1 = 10
0 • 8 = 0	4 • 0 = 0	18 ÷ 3 = 6	4 ÷ 2 = 2
4 * 9 = 36	9 * 5 = 40	12 ÷ 4 = 3	21 ÷ 3 = 7
2 × 0 = 0	4 × 9 = 36	40 / 5 = 8	8 / 4 = 2
1 • 3 = 3	10 • 5 = 50	36 ÷ 9 = 4	25 ÷ 5 = 5

Homework 4-16

Find the missing numbers. Then check your answers at the bottom of this page.

1. $6 \times 3 = \square$
2. $8 \div 2 = \square$
3. $5 * 0 = \square$
4. $4 / 2 = \square$
5. $3 \cdot \square = 6$
6. $\dfrac{7}{1} = \square$
7. $9 \times 1 = \square$
8. $\dfrac{0}{5} = \square$
9. $1 \times 6 = \square$
10. $4\overline{)8}$
11. $6 \cdot 4 = \square$
12. $0 \div 4 = \square$
13. $5 * \square = 10$
14. $\dfrac{9}{1} = \square$
15. $0 \cdot 1 = \square$
16. $\dfrac{25}{5} = \square$
17. $2 \div 2 = \square$
18. $8 * 2 = \square$
19. $\square \times 7 = 0$
20. $3\overline{)18}$
21. $1 * \square = 8$
22. $\square \times 3 = 9$
23. $4 \cdot 9 = \square$
24. $3 \div 1 = \square$

1. 18 2. 4 3. 0 4. 2 5. 2 6. 7 7. 9 8. 0 9. 6 10. 2
11. 24 12. 0 13. 2 14. 9 15. 0 16. 5 17. 1 18. 16 19. 0
20. 6 21. 8 22. 3 23. 36 24. 3

Practice with 0s, 1s, 2s, 3s, 4s, 5s, 9s, and 10s

4-16

Name _____ **Date** _____

Homework

Study Plan

_____
Homework Helper

Solve each problem.

1. Maili rode her bike 10 miles every day for 5 days. How many miles did she ride?

   _____

2. Leslie gave 72 balloons to children at the fair. After the fair, she had 9 balloons left. How many balloons did Leslie start with?

   _____

3. Tony hung some photographs on one wall in his room. He hung them in 3 rows, with 4 photos in each row. How many photos did Tony hang?

   _____

4. Pepe sent 15 gifts to his family members. He sent an equal amount of gifts to 3 different addresses. How many gifts did he send to each address?

   _____

5. At the Shady Acres Stables, there are 5 horses in each barn. There are 4 barns. How many horses are at Shady Acres?

   _____

6. Sixty students are in the marching band. There are 10 rows. How many students are in each row?

   _____

7. Danielle has 35 dolls in her collection. She wants to display them on 5 shelves. How many dolls should she put on each shelf?

   _____

8. There are 9 players on a baseball team. There are 6 teams in the league. How many baseball players are in the league?

   _____

UNIT 4 LESSON 16   Practice with 0s, 1s, 2s, 3s, 4s, 5s, 9s, and 10s **191**

4-16

Remembering

Solve each problem.

1. How many ears are on 6 dogs? Find the total by starting with the fifth count-by and counting up from there.

   _____

2. How many pancakes are in these 7 stacks? Find the total by starting with the fifth count-by and counting up from there.

   _____

Complete.

3. Find the area of the large rectangle by finding the areas of the two small rectangles and adding them.

   _____

4. Find the area of the large rectangle by multiplying the number of rows by the number of square units in each row.

   _____

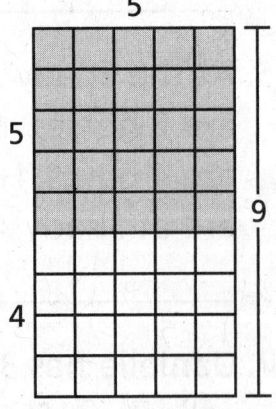

5. Find this product: 3 × 6 = _____

6. Find this product: 4 × 6 = _____

7. Use your answers to exercises 5 and 6 to find this product: 7 × 6 = _____

192 UNIT 4 LESSON 16   Practice with 0s, 1s, 2s, 3s, 4s, 5s, 9s, and 10s

D-2 Homework

Complete.

1. On a centimeter dot array, draw all possible rectangles with a perimeter of 16 cm and sides whose lengths are whole centimeters. Label the lengths of two adjacent sides of each rectangle.

2. Find and label the area of each rectangle. Then complete the table.

3. Compare the shapes of the rectangles with the least and greatest areas.

Rectangles with Perimeter 16 cm

Lengths of Two Adjacent Sides	Area

_____

4. On a centimeter dot array, draw all possible rectangles with an area of 16 sq cm and sides whose lengths are whole centimeters. Label the lengths of two adjacent sides of each rectangle.

5. Find and label the perimeter of each rectangle. Then complete the table.

Rectangles with Area 16 sq cm

Lengths of Two Adjacent Sides	Perimeter

6. Compare the shapes of the rectangles with the least and greatest perimeters.

_____

D-2 Remembering

Find each product.

1. 8 × ___ = _____
2. 5 × 2 = _____
3. 4 × 3 = _____
4. 2 × 9 = _____
5. 0 × 2 = _____
6. 3 × 7 = _____
7. ___ × 4 = _____
8. 3 × 3 = _____
9. 10 × 5 = _____

Find each quotient.

10. 10 ÷ 2 = _____
11. 9 ÷ 3 = _____
12. 5 ÷ 5 = _____
13. 7 ÷ 1 = _____
14. 10 ÷ 5 = _____
15. 8 ÷ 2 = _____

Solve each problem.

16. Margaret placed her horse-sticker collection in an album in 5 rows of 6. How many horse stickers does she have in her collection?

_____

17. Bower's Grocery Store has 9 shopping aisles. There are 8 shelves in each aisle. How many shelves are in the store?

_____

18. Mrs. Irving had 40 colored pencils for a graphing project. She gave 5 pencils to each student. How many students received pencils?

_____

Find the measure of the unknown angle in each triangle.

19.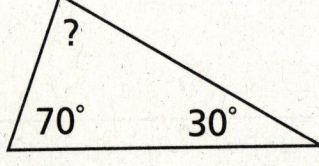

20.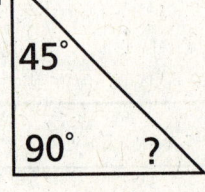

21.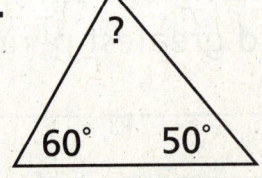

D-3 Homework

Find the area and perimeter of each rectangle.

1.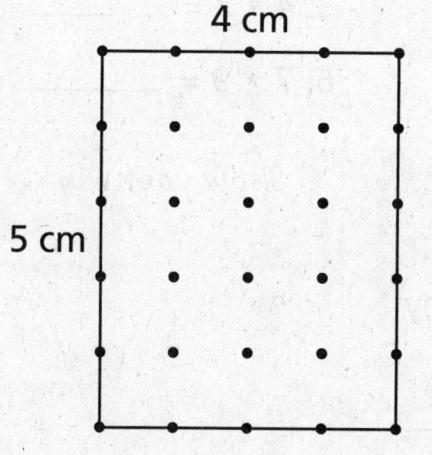

   Perimeter = _____

   Area = _____

2.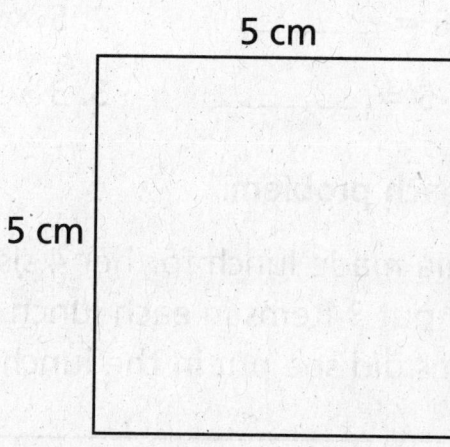

   Perimeter = _____

   Area = _____

Solve each problem.

Show your work.

3. Elbert wants to plant grass seed in his backyard. His yard is shaped like a rectangle that is 6 meters by 7 meters. He plans to use a cup of seed for every square meter in his yard. How many cups of grass seed will he need?

   _____

4. Serena has a square-shaped garden. She wants to put a fence around the outside of the garden. One side of the garden is 8 feet long. How many feet of fence will she need?

   _____

5. Ella has a rectangular quilt that is 4 feet wide and 6 feet long. What is the perimeter of her quilt?

   _____

6. A rectangular room is 9 feet long and 8 feet wide. What is the area of the room?

   _____

UNIT D LESSON 3   Formulas for Area and Perimeter **197**

D-3 Remembering

Find each product.

1. 3 • 6 = _____
2. 5 × 9 = _____
3. 4 • 3 = _____
4. 9 × 5 = _____
5. 3 * 9 = _____
6. 7 * 9 = _____

Solve each problem.   Show your work.

7. Paula made lunch for her 4 sisters and herself. She put 3 items in each lunch bag. How many items did she put in the lunch bags in all?

   _____

8. Jordan divided 72 marbles among his 9 friends. How many marbles did he give to each friend?

   _____

9. Hillary bought a sheet of 24 stamps. The sheet had 3 rows of stamps. How many stamps were in each row?

   _____

Write whether each pair of lines is parallel, perpendicular, or neither.

10.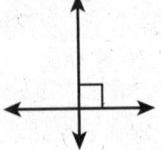
11.
12.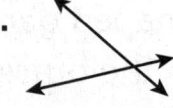
13.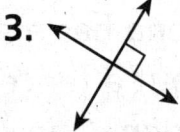

_____   _____   _____   _____

14. Name two parallel opposite sides in this figure.

    _____

15. Name two perpendicular adjacent sides.

    _____

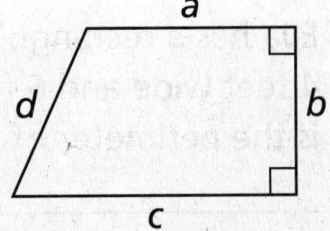

198 UNIT D LESSON 3   Formulas for Area and Perimeter

5-1 Homework   Name   Date

Use this chart to practice your 6 count-bys, multiplications, and divisions. Then have your Homework Helper test you.

	× In Order	× Mixed Up	÷ Mixed Up
6s	1 × 6 = 6	2 × 6 = 12	18 ÷ 6 = 3
	2 × 6 = 12	8 × 6 = 48	60 ÷ 6 = 10
	3 × 6 = 18	5 × 6 = 30	30 ÷ 6 = 5
	4 × 6 = 24	9 × 6 = 54	48 ÷ 6 = 8
	5 × 6 = 30	1 × 6 = 6	12 ÷ 6 = 2
	6 × 6 = 36	7 × 6 = 42	6 ÷ 6 = 1
	7 × 6 = 42	4 × 6 = 24	36 ÷ 6 = 6
	8 × 6 = 48	3 × 6 = 18	24 ÷ 6 = 4
	9 × 6 = 54	10 × 6 = 60	54 ÷ 6 = 9
	10 × 6 = 60	6 × 6 = 36	42 ÷ 6 = 7

5-1 Homework

Name _____ Date _____

Multiply or divide to find the missing numbers. Then check your answers at the bottom of this page.

1. $5 \times 5 = \square$
2. $12 \div 6 = \square$
3. $7 * 4 = \square$

4. $42 / 6 = \square$
5. $6 \cdot \square = 48$
6. $\frac{6}{1} = \square$

7. $10 \times 6 = \square$
8. $9\overline{)27}$ (quotient $\square$)
9. $6 \times 0 = \square$

10. $20 / 4 = \square$
11. $6 \cdot 6 = \square$
12. $18 \div 3 = \square$

13. $9 * \square = 54$
14. $\frac{60}{6} = \square$
15. $2 \cdot 7 = \square$

16. $16 / 4 = \square$
17. $6 \div 6 = \square$
18. $6 * 7 = \square$

19. $\square \times 7 = 0$
20. $9\overline{)45}$ (quotient $\square$)
21. $1 \times \square = 10$

Answers (upside down at bottom):
1. 25 2. 2 3. 28 4. 7 5. 8 6. 6 7. 60 8. 3 9. 0 10. 5 11. 36 12. 6 13. 6 14. 10 15. 14 16. 4 17. 1 18. 42 19. 0 20. 5 21. 10

200 UNIT 5 LESSON 1 — Multiply and Divide with 6

5-2 Homework

Home Study Sheet C

6s

Count-bys	Mixed Up ×	Mixed Up ÷
1 × 6 = 6	10 × 6 = 60	54 ÷ 6 = 9
2 × 6 = 12	8 × 6 = 48	30 ÷ 6 = 5
3 × 6 = 18	2 × 6 = 12	12 ÷ 6 = 2
4 × 6 = 24	6 × 6 = 36	60 ÷ 6 = 10
5 × 6 = 30	4 × 6 = 24	48 ÷ 6 = 8
6 × 6 = 36	1 × 6 = 6	36 ÷ 6 = 6
7 × 6 = 42	9 × 6 = 54	6 ÷ 6 = 1
8 × 6 = 48	3 × 6 = 18	42 ÷ 6 = 7
9 × 6 = 54	7 × 6 = 42	18 ÷ 6 = 3
10 × 6 = 60	5 × 6 = 30	24 ÷ 6 = 4

7s

Count-bys	Mixed Up ×	Mixed Up ÷
1 × 7 = 7	6 × 7 = 42	70 ÷ 7 = 10
2 × 7 = 14	8 × 7 = 56	14 ÷ 7 = 2
3 × 7 = 21	5 × 7 = 35	28 ÷ 7 = 4
4 × 7 = 28	9 × 7 = 63	56 ÷ 7 = 8
5 × 7 = 35	4 × 7 = 28	42 ÷ 7 = 6
6 × 7 = 42	10 × 7 = 70	63 ÷ 7 = 9
7 × 7 = 49	3 × 7 = 21	21 ÷ 7 = 3
8 × 7 = 56	1 × 7 = 7	49 ÷ 7 = 7
9 × 7 = 63	7 × 7 = 49	7 ÷ 7 = 1
10 × 7 = 70	2 × 7 = 14	35 ÷ 7 = 5

8s

Count-bys	Mixed Up ×	Mixed Up ÷
1 × 8 = 8	6 × 8 = 48	16 ÷ 8 = 2
2 × 8 = 16	10 × 8 = 80	40 ÷ 8 = 5
3 × 8 = 24	7 × 8 = 56	72 ÷ 8 = 9
4 × 8 = 32	2 × 8 = 16	32 ÷ 8 = 4
5 × 8 = 40	4 × 8 = 32	8 ÷ 8 = 1
6 × 8 = 48	8 × 8 = 64	80 ÷ 8 = 10
7 × 8 = 56	5 × 8 = 40	64 ÷ 8 = 8
8 × 8 = 64	10 × 8 = 80	24 ÷ 8 = 3
9 × 8 = 72	3 × 8 = 24	56 ÷ 8 = 7
10 × 8 = 80	1 × 8 = 8	48 ÷ 8 = 6

squares

Count-bys	Mixed Up ×	Mixed Up ÷
1 × 1 = 1	3 × 3 = 9	25 ÷ 5 = 5
2 × 2 = 4	9 × 9 = 81	4 ÷ 2 = 2
3 × 3 = 9	4 × 4 = 16	81 ÷ 9 = 9
4 × 4 = 16	6 × 6 = 36	9 ÷ 3 = 3
5 × 5 = 25	2 × 2 = 4	36 ÷ 6 = 6
6 × 6 = 36	7 × 7 = 49	100 ÷ 10 = 10
7 × 7 = 49	10 × 10 = 100	16 ÷ 4 = 4
8 × 8 = 64	1 × 1 = 1	49 ÷ 7 = 7
9 × 9 = 81	5 × 5 = 25	1 ÷ 1 = 1
10 × 10 = 100	8 × 8 = 64	64 ÷ 8 = 8

UNIT 5 LESSON 2

Home Study Sheet C **203**

Homework 5-2

Multiply or divide to find the missing numbers. Then check your answers at the bottom of this page.

1. 6 × 6 = ☐
2. 20 ÷ 4 = ☐
3. 9 * 9 = ☐
4. 32 / 4 = ☐
5. 9 • ☐ = 54
6. $\frac{30}{10}$ = ☐
7. 5 × 0 = ☐
8. $\frac{48}{6}$ = ☐
9. 3 × 6 = ☐
10. 6)̄30 (quotient ☐)
11. 8 • 4 = ☐
12. 12 ÷ 6 = ☐
13. 6 * ☐ = 42
14. $\frac{6}{6}$ = ☐
15. 3 • 4 = ☐
16. 15 / 5 = ☐
17. 10 ÷ 10 = ☐
18. 2 * 7 = ☐
19. ☐ × 2 = 10
20. 6)̄18 (quotient ☐)
21. 10 × ☐ = 70

1. 36 2. 5 3. 81 4. 8 5. 6 6. 3 7. 0 8. 8 9. 18 10. 5 11. 32 12. 2 13. 7 14. 1 15. 12 16. 3 17. 1 18. 14 19. 5 20. 3 21. 7

204 UNIT 5 LESSON 2   Solve Area Word Problems

Homework 5-3

Use this chart to practice your 8s count-bys, multiplications, and divisions. Then have your Homework Helper test you.

8s	× In Order	× Mixed Up	÷ Mixed Up
	1 × 8 = 8	3 × 8 = 24	40 ÷ 8 = 5
	2 × 8 = 16	9 × 8 = 72	56 ÷ 8 = 7
	3 × 8 = 24	6 × 8 = 48	24 ÷ 8 = 3
	4 × 8 = 32	4 × 8 = 32	72 ÷ 8 = 9
	5 × 8 = 40	2 × 8 = 16	8 ÷ 8 = 1
	6 × 8 = 48	8 × 8 = 64	48 ÷ 8 = 6
	7 × 8 = 56	1 × 8 = 8	32 ÷ 8 = 4
	8 × 8 = 64	5 × 8 = 40	64 ÷ 8 = 8
	9 × 8 = 72	10 × 8 = 80	16 ÷ 8 = 2
	10 × 8 = 80	7 × 8 = 56	80 ÷ 8 = 10

Home Check Sheet 8: 6s and 8s

6s Multiplications	6s Divisions	8s Multiplications	8s Divisions
10 × 6 = 60	24 / 6 = 4	2 × 8 = 16	72 / 8 = 9
6 • 4 = 24	48 ÷ 6 = 8	8 • 10 = 80	16 ÷ 8 = 2
6 * 7 = 42	60 / 6 = 10	3 * 8 = 24	40 / 8 = 5
2 × 6 = 12	12 ÷ 6 = 2	9 × 8 = 72	8 ÷ 8 = 1
6 • 5 = 30	42 / 6 = 7	8 • 4 = 32	80 / 8 = 10
6 * 8 = 48	30 ÷ 6 = 5	8 * 7 = 56	48 ÷ 8 = 6
9 × 6 = 54	6 / 6 = 1	5 × 8 = 40	56 / 8 = 7
6 • 1 = 6	18 ÷ 6 = 3	8 • 6 = 48	24 ÷ 8 = 3
6 * 6 = 36	54 / 6 = 9	1 * 8 = 8	64 / 8 = 8
6 × 3 = 18	36 / 6 = 6	8 × 8 = 64	32 / 8 = 4
6 • 6 = 36	48 ÷ 6 = 8	4 • 8 = 32	80 ÷ 8 = 10
5 * 6 = 30	12 / 6 = 2	6 * 8 = 48	56 / 8 = 7
6 × 2 = 12	24 ÷ 6 = 4	8 × 3 = 24	8 ÷ 8 = 1
4 • 6 = 24	60 / 6 = 10	7 • 8 = 56	24 / 8 = 3
6 * 9 = 54	6 ÷ 6 = 1	8 * 2 = 16	64 ÷ 8 = 8
8 × 6 = 48	42 / 6 = 7	8 × 9 = 72	16 ÷ 8 = 2
7 • 6 = 42	18 ÷ 6 = 3	8 • 1 = 8	72 ÷ 8 = 9
6 * 10 = 60	36 ÷ 6 = 6	8 * 8 = 64	32 ÷ 8 = 4
1 × 6 = 6	30 / 6 = 5	10 × 8 = 80	40 / 8 = 5
4 • 6 = 24	54 ÷ 6 = 9	5 • 8 = 40	48 ÷ 8 = 6

5-4 Homework

Study Plan

Homework Helper

Solve. Then circle what type it is and what operation you used.

1. The area of a photograph is 15 square inches. If the width of the photograph is 3 inches, what is its length?

   _____

   array   repeated groups   area

   multiplication   division

2. Mrs. Divita divided 64 beetles equally among the 8 students in the science club. How many beetles did each student receive?

   _____

   array   repeated groups   area

   multiplication   division

3. Write your own problem that is the same type as problem 1.

   _____
   _____
   _____

4. Write your own problem that is the same type as problem 2.

   _____
   _____
   _____

Find the missing number in each Fast-Array Drawing.

5.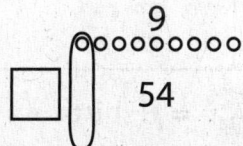

6.

7.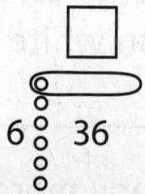

UNIT 5 LESSON 4   Write Word Problems **211**

5-4 Remembering

Draw the lines of symmetry for each figure.

1.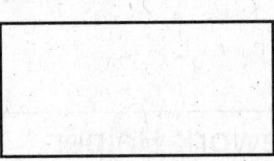

2.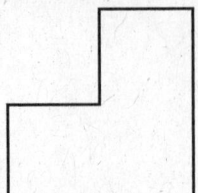

3.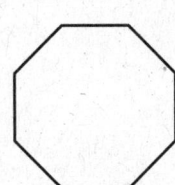

Use the angles at the right to answer questions 4–6.

4. Which of the angles are right angles?
   _____

5. Which of the angles are smaller than a right angle?
   _____

6. Which of the angles are larger than a right angle?
   _____

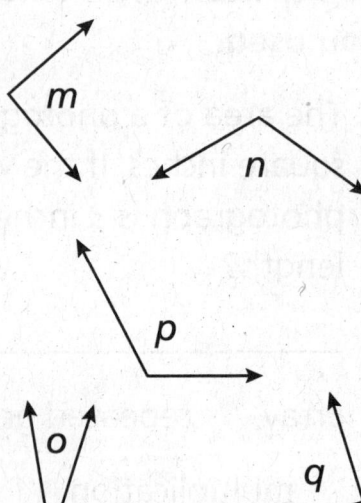

Use the graph to answer questions 7–10.

7. How many blue T-shirts were sold?
   _____

8. How many white and green T-shirts were sold altogether?
   _____

9. How many fewer red T-shirts were sold than white T-shirts?
   _____

10. How many more blue T-shirts were sold than red T-shirts?
    _____

T-Shirt Sales

White	🎽🎽🎽🎽🎽
Red	🎽🎽
Blue	🎽🎽🎽🎽
Green	🎽🎽🎽

Key: 🎽 = 6 shirts

5-5 Homework

Name _____ **Date** _____

Use this chart to practice your 7s count-bys, multiplications, and divisions. Then have your Homework Helper test you.

7s

× In Order	× Mixed Up	÷ Mixed Up
1 × 7 = 7	5 × 7 = 35	56 ÷ 7 = 8
2 × 7 = 14	1 × 7 = 7	42 ÷ 7 = 6
3 × 7 = 21	10 × 7 = 70	14 ÷ 7 = 2
4 × 7 = 28	2 × 7 = 14	7 ÷ 7 = 1
5 × 7 = 35	9 × 7 = 63	70 ÷ 7 = 10
6 × 7 = 42	3 × 7 = 21	49 ÷ 7 = 7
7 × 7 = 49	8 × 7 = 56	21 ÷ 7 = 3
8 × 7 = 56	4 × 7 = 28	35 ÷ 7 = 5
9 × 7 = 63	7 × 7 = 49	63 ÷ 7 = 9
10 × 7 = 70	6 × 7 = 42	28 ÷ 7 = 4

5-5 Homework

Name _____ **Date** _____

Multiply or divide to find the missing numbers. Then check your answers at the bottom of this page.

1. $7 \times 7 = \square$
2. $\dfrac{64}{8} = \square$
3. $5 \times 5 = \square$

4. $28 / 7 = \square$
5. $9 \cdot \square = 27$
6. $\dfrac{48}{6} = \square$

7. $\square \times 9 = 63$
8. $7\overline{)56}$ with $\square$ on top
9. $10 \times \square = 30$

10. $8 \times 5 = \square$
11. $21 \div 3 = \square$
12. $9 * 2 = \square$

13. $30 / 6 = \square$
14. $8 \cdot 5 = \square$
15. $24 \div 3 = \square$

16. $3\overline{)21}$ with $\square$ on top
17. $90 \div 9 = \square$
18. $2 * 7 = \square$

19. $6 * \square = 42$
20. $\dfrac{10}{2} = \square$
21. $3 \cdot 9 = \square$

---

1. 49 2. 8 3. 25 4. 3 5. 3 6. 8 7. 7 8. 8 9. 3 10. 40 11. 7 12. 18 13. 5 14. 40 15. 8 16. 7 17. 10 18. 14 19. 7 20. 5 21. 27

214 UNIT 5 LESSON 5 — Multiply and Divide with 7

5-7 Homework

Study Plan

Homework Helper

Complete the sentence.

> Kristi is training for a marathon. This month she ran 36 miles. Last month she ran only 6 miles.

1. Kristi ran _____ as many miles this month as last month.

2. Kristi ran _____ as many miles last month as this month.

Make a drawing to help you solve each problem.

3. Darnell swam 8 miles last month. He plans to swim 3 times as many miles this month. How many miles does he plan to swim this month?
_____

4. Geoff rode 64 miles on his bike last month. He rode $\frac{1}{8}$ as many miles this month as last month. How many miles did he ride this month?
_____

5. Molly ran in 4 races at the track meet. Her sister Sophie ran in 8 races. How many more races did Sophie run in than Molly? _____

6. Tamara made 8 baskets in the championship game. Lucia made $\frac{1}{4}$ as many baskets as Tamara. How many baskets did Lucia make? _____

Show your work.

UNIT 5 LESSON 7 More Comparison Word Problems 219

5-7 Remembering

Subtract.

1. 408 − 275 = _____
2. 129 − 63 = _____
3. 472 − 319 = _____

4. 647 − 118 = _____
5. 727 − 144 = _____
6. 300 − 17 = _____

Find the area and perimeter of each rectangle.

7. 7 ft / 3 ft

8. 5 cm / 4 cm

9. 6 in. / 6 in.

10. 2 ft / 10 ft

11. 3 cm / 7 cm

12. 7 in. / 9 in.

220 UNIT 5 LESSON 7 — More Comparison Word Problems

Home Check Sheet 9: 7s and Squares

7s Multiplications	7s Divisions	Squares Multiplications	Squares Divisions
4 × 7 = 28	14 / 7 = 2	8 × 8 = 64	81 / 9 = 9
7 • 2 = 14	28 ÷ 7 = 4	10 • 10 = 100	4 ÷ 2 = 2
7 * 8 = 56	70 / 7 = 10	3 * 3 = 9	25 / 5 = 5
7 × 7 = 49	56 ÷ 7 = 8	9 × 9 = 81	1 ÷ 1 = 1
7 • 1 = 7	42 / 7 = 6	4 • 4 = 16	100 / 10 = 10
7 * 10 = 70	63 ÷ 7 = 9	7 * 7 = 49	36 ÷ 6 = 6
3 × 7 = 21	7 / 7 = 1	5 × 5 = 25	49 / 7 = 7
7 • 6 = 42	49 ÷ 7 = 7	6 • 6 = 36	9 ÷ 3 = 3
5 * 7 = 35	21 / 7 = 3	1 * 1 = 1	64 / 8 = 8
7 × 9 = 63	35 / 7 = 5	5 * 5 = 25	16 / 4 = 4
7 • 4 = 28	7 ÷ 7 = 1	1 • 1 = 1	100 ÷ 10 = 10
9 * 7 = 63	63 / 7 = 9	3 • 3 = 9	49 / 7 = 7
2 × 7 = 14	14 ÷ 7 = 2	10 × 10 = 100	1 ÷ 1 = 1
7 • 5 = 35	70 / 7 = 10	4 × 4 = 16	9 / 3 = 3
8 * 7 = 56	21 ÷ 7 = 3	9 * 9 = 81	64 ÷ 8 = 8
7 × 3 = 21	49 / 7 = 7	2 × 2 = 4	4 / 2 = 2
6 • 7 = 42	28 ÷ 7 = 4	6 * 6 = 36	81 ÷ 9 = 9
10 * 7 = 70	56 ÷ 7 = 8	7 × 7 = 49	16 ÷ 4 = 4
1 × 7 = 7	35 / 7 = 5	5 • 5 = 25	25 / 5 = 5
7 • 7 = 49	42 ÷ 7 = 6	8 • 8 = 64	36 ÷ 6 = 6

5-8 Homework

Multiply or divide to find the missing numbers. Then check your answers at the bottom of this page.

1. ☐ × 6 = 48
2. 56 ÷ 7 = ☐
3. 10 × ☐ = 90

4. 64 / 8 = ☐
5. 9 • ☐ = 63
6. $\frac{25}{5}$ = ☐

7. 8 × 9 = ☐
8. 9)☐̄36
9. 7 * 7 = ☐

10. 6 * ☐ = 36
11. $\frac{32}{4}$ = ☐
12. 3 • 3 = ☐

13. 30 / 6 = ☐
14. 16 ÷ 4 = ☐
15. 8 * 5 = ☐

16. 6 × 4 = ☐
17. $\frac{81}{9}$ = ☐
18. 5 × 7 = ☐

19. 60 / 6 = ☐
20. 7 • 8 = ☐
21. 42 ÷ 7 = ☐

22. 6)☐̄54
23. 32 ÷ 8 = ☐
24. 9 * 9 = ☐

1. 8 2. 8 3. 9 4. 8 5. 7 6. 5 7. 72 8. 4 9. 49 10. 6 11. 8 12. 9
13. 5 14. 4 15. 40 16. 24 17. 9 18. 35 19. 10 20. 56 21. 6 22. 9 23. 4 24. 81

222 UNIT 5 LESSON 8

Square Numbers

5-8 Homework

Study Plan

Homework Helper

Write a multiplication equation for each square array.

   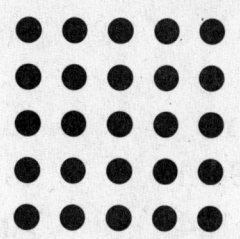   

1. _____ 2. _____ 3. _____

Solve.

4. Julia used 1 foot square stone tiles to make a patio. She laid the tiles in a square, 7 tiles wide by 7 tiles long. What is the area of Julia's new patio?

_____

5. Sal brought 2 dozen apples to a science club meeting. He divided the apples equally among the 8 people there. How many apples did he give each person?

_____

6. Lehie has 21 crystals in her collection. Her brother Tomer has 7 crystals. How many more crystals does Lehie have than Tomer?

_____

7. Emmanuel collected 49 leaves last week. He collected the same number of leaves each day. How many leaves did he collect on Monday?

_____

Complete.

8.

×	6	4	
	24		32

9.

×		4	
9	45		81

10.

×	8		3
8		56	

UNIT 5 LESSON 8 — Square Numbers 223

5-8 Remembering

Solve.

1. Isabel had $37. She bought 2 CDs for $11 each. Then she earned some money babysitting. Now she has $53. How much did she earn babysitting?

2. Arnon planted 4 apple trees and 7 peach trees. Jenn planted 5 more apple trees than Arnon and 4 fewer peach trees. How many trees did Jenn plant in all?

3. Brigitte scored 234 points in a pinball game. Lee scored 394. In a second game, Lee scored 164 points, and Brigitte scored 307 points. Altogether, who scored the most points? How many more?

4. Julian caught 8 fish, Tana caught 6, Stewart caught 11, and Ana caught 4. They threw the 9 smallest fish back into the water. Then they each caught 2 more fish. How many fish do they have now?

Draw 2 figures that each have a perimeter of 12 centimeters. Write the area inside each figure.

5.

Home Check Sheet 10: 6s, 7s, and 8s

6s, 7s, and 8s Multiplications	6s, 7s, and 8s Multiplications	6s, 7s, and 8s Divisions	6s, 7s, and 8s Divisions
1 × 6 = 6	0 × 8 = 0	24 / 6 = 4	54 / 6 = 9
6 • 7 = 42	6 • 2 = 12	21 ÷ 7 = 3	24 ÷ 8 = 3
3 * 8 = 24	4 * 7 = 28	16 / 8 = 2	14 / 7 = 2
6 × 2 = 12	8 × 3 = 24	24 ÷ 8 = 3	32 ÷ 8 = 4
7 • 5 = 35	5 • 6 = 30	14 / 7 = 2	18 / 6 = 3
8 * 4 = 32	7 * 2 = 14	30 ÷ 6 = 5	56 ÷ 7 = 8
6 × 6 = 36	3 × 8 = 24	35 / 7 = 5	40 / 8 = 5
8 • 7 = 56	6 • 4 = 24	24 ÷ 8 = 3	35 ÷ 7 = 5
9 * 8 = 72	0 * 7 = 0	18 / 6 = 3	12 / 6 = 2
6 × 10 = 60	8 × 1 = 8	12 / 6 = 2	21 / 7 = 3
7 • 1 = 7	8 • 6 = 48	42 ÷ 7 = 6	16 ÷ 8 = 2
8 * 3 = 24	7 * 9 = 63	56 / 8 = 7	42 / 6 = 7
5 × 6 = 30	10 × 8 = 80	49 ÷ 7 = 7	80 ÷ 8 = 10
4 • 7 = 28	6 • 10 = 60	16 / 8 = 2	36 / 6 = 6
2 * 8 = 16	3 * 7 = 21	60 ÷ 6 = 10	7 ÷ 7 = 1
7 × 7 = 49	8 × 4 = 32	54 / 6 = 9	64 / 8 = 8
7 • 6 = 42	6 • 5 = 30	8 ÷ 8 = 1	24 ÷ 6 = 4
8 * 8 = 64	7 * 4 = 28	28 ÷ 7 = 4	21 ÷ 7 = 3
9 × 6 = 54	8 × 8 = 64	72 / 8 = 9	49 / 7 = 7
10 • 7 = 70	6 • 9 = 54	56 ÷ 7 = 8	24 ÷ 8 = 3

5-9 Homework

Name   Date

Home Check Sheet 11: 0s–10s

0s–10s Multiplications	0s–10s Multiplications	0s–10s Divisions	0s–10s Divisions
9 × 0 = 0	9 × 4 = 36	9 / 1 = 9	90 / 10 = 9
1 • 1 = 1	5 • 9 = 45	12 ÷ 3 = 4	64 ÷ 8 = 8
2 * 3 = 6	6 * 10 = 60	14 / 2 = 7	15 / 5 = 3
1 × 3 = 3	7 × 3 = 21	20 ÷ 4 = 5	12 ÷ 6 = 2
5 • 4 = 20	5 • 3 = 15	10 / 5 = 2	14 / 7 = 2
7 * 5 = 35	4 * 1 = 4	48 ÷ 8 = 6	45 ÷ 9 = 5
6 × 9 = 54	7 × 5 = 35	35 / 7 = 5	8 / 1 = 8
0 • 7 = 0	6 • 3 = 18	60 ÷ 6 = 10	30 ÷ 3 = 10
1 * 8 = 8	8 * 7 = 56	81 / 9 = 9	16 / 4 = 4
9 × 8 = 72	5 × 8 = 40	20 / 10 = 2	8 / 2 = 4
2 • 10 = 20	9 • 9 = 81	16 ÷ 2 = 8	80 ÷ 10 = 8
0 * 7 = 0	9 * 10 = 90	30 / 5 = 6	36 / 4 = 9
4 × 1 = 4	0 × 0 = 0	49 ÷ 7 = 7	25 ÷ 5 = 5
2 • 4 = 8	1 • 0 = 0	60 / 6 = 10	42 / 7 = 6
10 * 3 = 30	1 * 6 = 6	30 ÷ 3 = 10	36 ÷ 6 = 6
8 × 4 = 32	7 × 2 = 14	8 / 1 = 8	90 / 9 = 10
5 • 8 = 40	6 • 3 = 18	16 ÷ 4 = 4	24 ÷ 8 = 3
4 * 6 = 24	4 * 5 = 20	16 ÷ 8 = 2	6 ÷ 2 = 3
7 × 0 = 0	6 × 6 = 36	40 / 10 = 4	9 / 3 = 3
1 • 8 = 8	10 • 7 = 70	36 ÷ 9 = 4	1 ÷ 1 = 1

5-11 Homework

Name _____ Date _____

Study Plan

Homework Helper

Solve each problem.

1. The tour boats at the Laguna can carry 8 passengers. Jacob watched 6 boats float by. Three of the boats had 2 empty seats. The others were full. How many passengers were on the 6 boats?

2. Jerome bought 8 packs of baseball cards at a garage sale. Each pack had 10 cards. He gave his younger sister 3 cards from each pack. How many cards does Jerome have left?

3. Zoe cut a pan of brownies into 5 rows and 6 columns. She gave 6 brownies to her family, and divided the rest evenly among the 8 people at her scout meeting. How many brownies did each person at her scout meeting get?

4. Four girls helped Mr. Day plant a garden. For their help, he gave the girls $24 to share equally. Later, Mrs. Day gave each girl $2 for helping to clean up. How much money did each girl get?

5. Grace made 7 bouquets for the bridesmaids in a wedding. She put 3 roses, 4 tulips, and 2 lilies in each bouquet. How many flowers did she use in all?

6. Takala put 9 marbles in the box, Jackie put in 7, and Laird put in 11. Then they divided the marbles evenly among themselves. How many did each person get?

UNIT 5 LESSON 11 Solve Multi-Step Word Problems **231**

5-11 Remembering

Solve each problem by rounding to the nearest hundred.

1. The population of Westville is 783. The population of Eastville is 327. About how many people live in the two towns altogether?

   _____

2. Of the 1,822 people who attended the county fair, 178 saw the horse show. About how many fairgoers did not see the horse show?

   _____

Use the graph to solve problems 3–8.

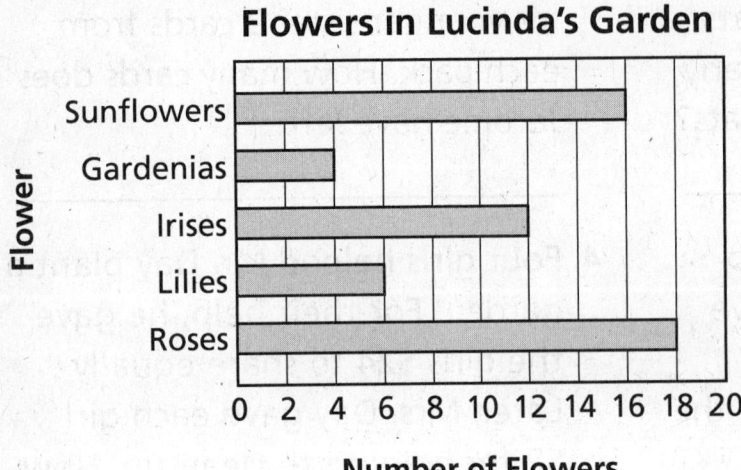

3. Lucinda has _____ as many roses as lilies.

4. Lucinda has _____ as many gardenias as irises.

5. Lucinda has _____ as many sunflowers as gardenias.

6. Lucinda has _____ as many lilies as irises.

7. Lucinda has _____ more irises than lilies.

8. Lucinda has _____ fewer gardenias than sunflowers.

E-1 Homework

Name _____ Date _____

Write the time on the digital clock. Then write how to say the time.

1.    2.    3.    4.

       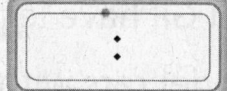   

_____   _____   _____   _____

Draw the hands on the anolog clock. Write the time on the digital clock.

5. twenty-eight minutes after four   **6.** six forty-five   **7.** quarter to seven

   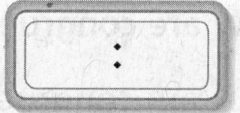   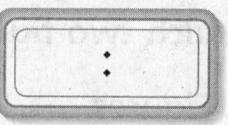

Write the time as minutes *after* an hour and minutes *before* an hour.

8.    **9.**    **10.**

_____   _____   _____

_____   _____   _____

UNIT E LESSON 1   Tell Time **237**

E-1 Remembering

Solve.

1. A theater has 8 rows of 9 seats. All the seats but 3 are full. How many people are in the audience? _____

2. Gil's scrapbook had 12 pages, each with 4 hockey cards in it. He gave 6 hockey cards to his brother. How many cards did Gil have left? _____

3. Odessa made 10 model cars with 4 wheels each. She had 8 wheels left over. How many wheels did she start with? _____

Draw all the possible lines of symmetry on each figure.

4.

5.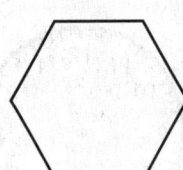

6.

Which two figures in each row are congruent?

7. Figures _____ and _____ are congruent.

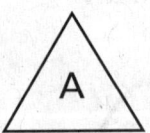 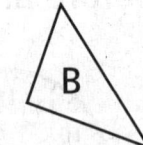 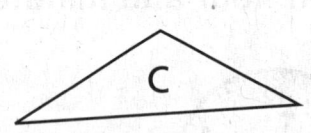 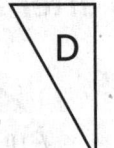 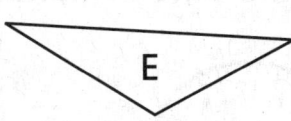

8. Figures _____ and _____ are congruent.

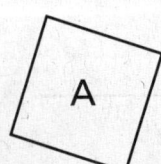 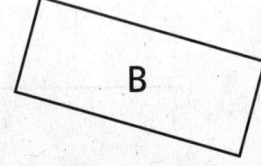 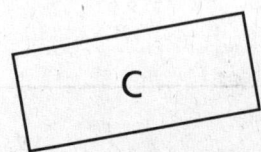 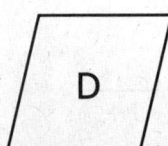

238 UNIT E LESSON 1 — Tell Time

E-3 Homework

These clocks show the movement of the minute hand.

Tell how many minutes have passed and how many degrees the minute hand has rotated.

1.
   minutes: _____
   degrees: _____

2.
   minutes: _____
   degrees: _____

3.
   minutes: _____
   degrees: _____

4.
   minutes: _____
   degrees: _____

The minute hand rotates 6 degrees(°) in one minute.

Complete.

5. From 3:33 to 3:42, _____ minutes pass.
   The minute hand rotates _____ degrees.

6. From 12:03 to 12:15, _____ minutes pass.
   The minute hand rotates _____ degrees.

7. From 1:57 to 2:08, _____ minutes pass.
   The minute hand rotates _____ degrees.

Solve.

8. A clock starts at 5:05. What time is it after the minute hand rotates 12°?
   _____

9. A clock starts at 12:59. What time is it after the minute hand rotates 24°?
   _____

10. A clock starts at 8:44. What time is it after the minute hand rotates 48°?
    _____

11. A clock starts at 1:00. What time is it after the minute hand rotates 36°?
    _____

UNIT E LESSON 3

Remembering

Find the missing number.

1. 7 × 4 = ☐
2. 49 ÷ 7 = ☐
3. ☐ * 6 = 54
4. 24 / 6 = ☐
5. 9 • ☐ = 27
6. 49 / 7 = ☐
7. ☐ × 5 = 45
8. ☐ / 4 = 8
9. 5 × ☐ = 40

Complete the Missing Number Puzzle.

10.

×	5	4	
	30		54
9		36	
	35		

11.

×		8	
6			42
8			56
		21	56

Write two letter names for each figure.

12.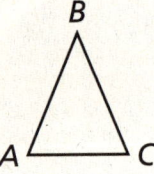
_____

13.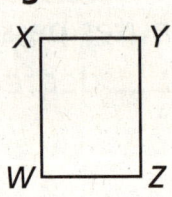
_____

14.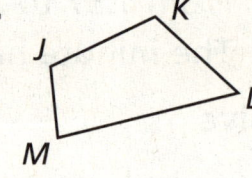
_____

Draw each figure if possible.

15. A rectangle that is not a square.

16. A parallelogram that is not a rectangle.

17. A quadrilateral that is not a parallelogram.

18. A rhombus that is not a parallelogram.

6-4 Homework

Use the bar graph at the right to fill in the blanks.

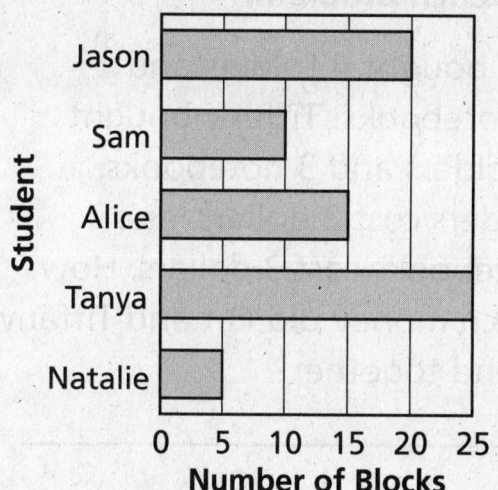

Number of Blocks Walked to School

1. Sam walks _____ as many blocks as Natalie walks.

   Natalie walks _____ as many blocks as Sam walks.

2. Alice walks _____ as many blocks as Natalie walks.

   Natalie walks _____ as many blocks as Alice walks.

3. Sam walks _____ as many blocks as Jason walks.

   Jason walks _____ as many blocks as Sam walks.

4. Natalie walks _____ as many blocks as Tanya walks.

   Tanya walks _____ as many blocks as Natalie walks.

5. Jason walks _____ as many blocks as Natalie walks.

   Natalie walks _____ as many blocks as Jason walks.

Solve each problem.

6. Wanda picked 27 apples at the Sunshine Farm. Her little brother Roy picked $\frac{1}{3}$ as many apples. How many apples did Roy pick?

   _____

7. Frankie has 7 baseball cards. Rika has 4 times as many baseball cards. How many baseball cards does Rika have?

   _____

UNIT 6 LESSON 4   Compare with Fractions **249**

Remembering

Solve each problem.

1. Pat bought 4 folders and 3 notebooks. Tiffany bought 2 folders and 3 notebooks. Folders cost 2 dollars, and notebooks cost 3 dollars. How much money did Pat and Tiffany spend together?

2. There are 3 pencils in an art box. There are 2 times as many markers as pencils. There are 3 times as many crayons as markers. How many pencils, markers, and crayons are in the box?

3. Marge bought 3 books of stamps. There were 9 stamps in each book. Then her mom gave her 46 stamps, and her dad gave her 12 stamps. She used 5 stamps to mail letters. How many stamps does Margaret have left?

4. Ilia walked 4 miles on Monday. He walked 3 times as far on Tuesday. On Tuesday, Anna walked half as far as Ilia walked on Tuesday. How far did Anna walk on Tuesday?

Draw hands on the analog clock. Write the time on the digital clock.

5. half-past 12

6. eight-twenty

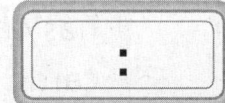

7. six-fifty

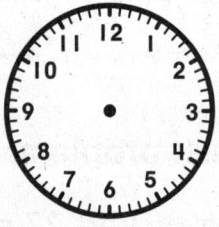

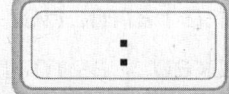

6-7 Homework

Complete.

1. Abbot and Maria baked 24 loaves of bread. Use the circle graph to complete the table.

Loaves of Bread Baked

Circle graph shows: $\frac{2}{6}$ white, $\frac{3}{8}$ wheat, $\frac{1}{8}$ rye, $\frac{1}{6}$ banana

	Fraction of Whole	Number of Loaves
White		
Rye		
Wheat		
Banana		

2. Did Abbot and Maria bake more banana or rye bread? How can you tell by looking at the graph?
   _____
   _____
   _____

3. Aaron and his classmates have a total of 48 pets. Aaron made a circle graph to show the kinds of pets his classmates have. Write a fraction in the circle graph for each kind of pet.

Students' Pets

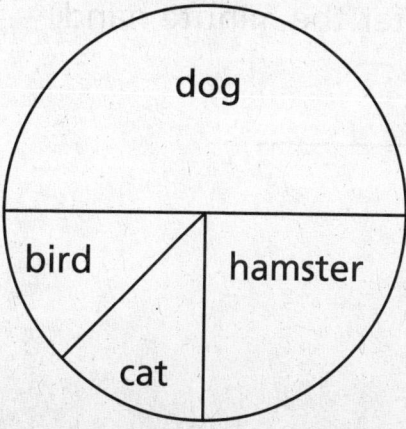

4. How many more dogs are there than cats?
   _____

UNIT 6 LESSON 7 — Fractions on Circle Graphs

6–7 Remembering

Find the area of each figure below.

1.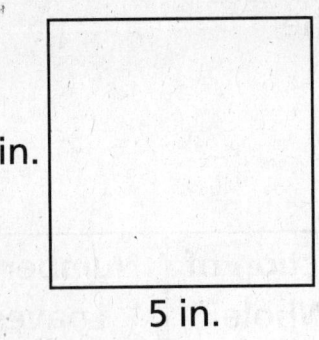

2.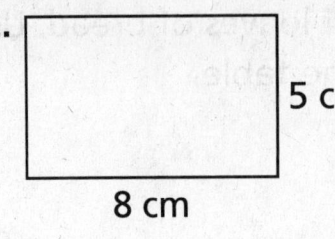

3.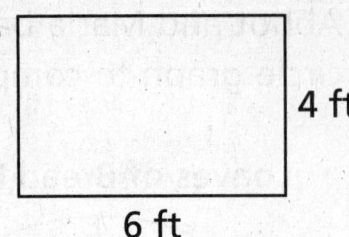

_____   _____   _____

4. Hal started his homework when he got home from school and worked until 4:45 P.M. He did homework for an hour and a half. What time did he start doing homework?

_____

5. Juanita practiced her flute from 3:30 to 4:00 P.M. each day Monday through Friday. How much time did she spend practicing her flute altogether on those days?

_____

6. A clock starts at 5:15 A.M. What time is it after the minute hand rotates 90°?

_____

7. It is 1:25 P.M. What time will it be when the minute hand rotates 180°?

_____

256 UNIT 6 LESSON 7   Fractions on Circle Graphs

6-9 Homework

Use your fraction strips for exercises 1–6. Fill in the blanks.

1. How many twelfths are in one fourth? _____

    Complete these equations:

    _____ twelfths = 1 fourth $\dfrac{\Box}{12} = \dfrac{1}{4}$

2. How many sixteenths are in one fourth? _____

    Complete these equations:

    _____ sixteenths = 1 fourth $\dfrac{\Box}{16} = \dfrac{1}{4}$

3. How many eighths are in three fourths? _____

    Complete these equations:

    _____ eighths = 3 fourths $\dfrac{\Box}{8} = \dfrac{3}{4}$

4. How many twelfths are in three fourths? _____

    Complete these equations:

    _____ twelfths = 3 fourths $\dfrac{\Box}{12} = \dfrac{3}{4}$

5. How many sixteenths are in three fourths? _____

    Complete these equations:

    _____ sixteenths = 3 fourths $\dfrac{\Box}{16} = \dfrac{3}{4}$

6. Find three other pairs of equivalent fractions.

_____   _____   _____

UNIT 6 LESSON 9   Introduce Equivalence 257

6-9 Remembering

Complete each Missing Number puzzle.

1.

×		7	6
5	40		
6			
		63	

2.

×	9	6	
7			
4			32
		27	

Flowers at the Flower Shop

3.

	$\frac{1}{5}$ white	$\frac{4}{5}$ not white
30 roses		
35 tulips		
45 carnations		
40 daisies		
20 lilies		

Items at the Clothing Store

4.

	$\frac{1}{8}$ blue	$\frac{7}{8}$ not blue
72 shirts		
24 jackets		
64 pairs of pants		
48 skirts		
56 caps		

258 UNIT 6 LESSON 9 Introduce Equivalence

6-10 Homework

Name _____ Date _____

Play *Spinning a Whole* with a friend or with a member of your family. Use the game boards and spinners that your teacher gave you. Here are the rules.

Rules for *Spinning a Whole*

Number of Players: 2 or 3

Materials: a game board and matching pair of spinners for each player, paper clips, ruler

1. On each turn, a player chooses and spins one of the two spinners.

2. Using the labeled fraction bars as a guide, the player marks and shades a section of the whole to represent the fraction the spinner landed on.

   - On a player's first turn, the player starts at the left end of the whole.
   - On other turns, the player starts at the right end of the last section shaded.

3. If a player spins a fraction greater than the unshaded portion of the whole, the player does not shade anything on his or her turn.

4. The first player to fill his or her whole bar completely and exactly wins.

Use the fraction bars on the *Spinning a Whole* game boards to fill in the blanks.

1. $\frac{1}{4} = \frac{\Box}{16}$

2. $\frac{1}{2} = \frac{\Box}{8}$

3. $\frac{5}{8} = \frac{\Box}{16}$

4. $\frac{1}{3} = \frac{\Box}{6}$

5. $\frac{5}{6} = \frac{\Box}{12}$

6. $\frac{2}{3} = \frac{\Box}{12}$

UNIT 6 LESSON 10   Explore Equivalence **259**

6–10

Remembering

Add or subtract.

1. $2.77
   + 4.25

2. 348
   + 867

3. 340
   − 209

4. $8.36
   + 9.41

5. $3.60
   − 2.17

6. 739
   + 279

7. 724
   − 687

8. $7.38
   − 4.45

Solve each problem.

Show your work.

> Chip earned $17 washing cars. His brother Dirk earned $32 raking leaves.

9. How much more money must Chip earn to have as much as Dirk?

_____

10. Dirk spent $\frac{1}{2}$ of his money on some new CDs. How much money does Dirk have now?

_____

> There are 3 black horses on the big merry-go-round, and 7 times as many white horses. There are 6 black horses on the small merry-go-round, and 4 times as many white horses.

11. Which merry-go-round has more white horses?

_____

12. How many more white horses does it have?

_____

Explore Equivalence

6-11 Homework

Complete.

1.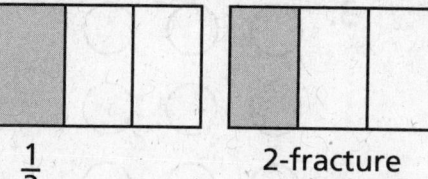
   $\frac{1}{3}$ 2-fracture each third

   $\frac{1}{3} \times \frac{\square}{\square} = \frac{\square}{\square}$

2.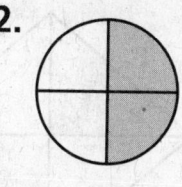
   $\frac{2}{4}$ 3-fracture each fourth

   $\frac{2}{4} \times \frac{\square}{\square} = \frac{\square}{\square}$

3.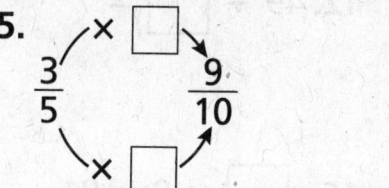
   $\frac{1}{2}$

   5-fracture each half

   $\frac{1}{2} = \frac{1}{2} \times \frac{\square}{\square} = \frac{\square}{\square}$

4.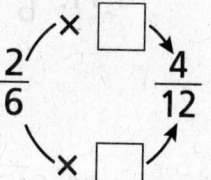
   $\frac{2}{3}$

   3-fracture each third

   $\frac{2}{3} = \frac{2}{3} \times \frac{\square}{\square} = \frac{\square}{\square}$

Write the multiplier in the box. Are the fractions equivalent? Write yes or no. If the fractions are equivalent, write the common multiplier.

5. $\frac{3}{5} \xrightarrow{\times \square} \frac{9}{10}$ $\xrightarrow{\times \square}$

   _____

6. $\frac{2}{6} \xrightarrow{\times \square} \frac{4}{12}$ $\xrightarrow{\times \square}$

   _____

7. $\frac{4}{5} \xrightarrow{\times \square} \frac{8}{10}$ $\xrightarrow{\times \square}$

   _____

8. $\frac{7}{8} \xrightarrow{\times \square} \frac{14}{24}$ $\xrightarrow{\times \square}$

   _____

9. $\frac{1}{2} \xrightarrow{\times \square} \frac{40}{80}$ $\xrightarrow{\times \square}$

   _____

10. $\frac{7}{8} \xrightarrow{\times \square} \frac{49}{56}$ $\xrightarrow{\times \square}$

    _____

UNIT 6 LESSON 11   Equivalence Patterns **261**

6–11 Remembering

Write a fraction to represent the part that is shaded.

1.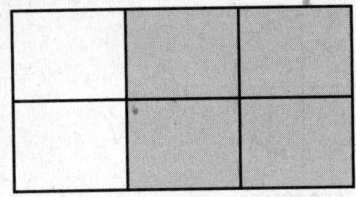

   _____ or _____

2.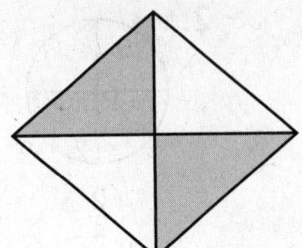

   _____ or _____

3.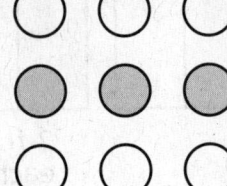

   _____ or _____

Multiply or divide to find the unknown number.

4. $7 \times \boxed{} = 56$

5. $36 \div 6 = \boxed{}$

6. $\boxed{} \cdot 8 = 32$

7. $\boxed{} / 9 = 7$

8. $5 \times 4 = \boxed{}$

9. $6\overline{)42}$ with $\boxed{}$ on top

10. $6 * \boxed{} = 24$

11. $\dfrac{\boxed{}}{6} = 8$

12. $49 \div \boxed{} = 7$

13. $9 \times \boxed{} = 54$

14. $8\overline{)\boxed{}}$ with 8 on top

15. $\boxed{} \times 9 = 81$

16. $4 \times 9 = \boxed{}$

17. $21 \div \boxed{} = 3$

18. $3 \times \boxed{} = 27$

Equivalence Patterns

6-12 Homework

Name _____ Date _____

Use the fraction strips to show how each pair is equivalent.

1. $\frac{1}{3}$ and $\frac{2}{6}$

$\frac{1}{3} = \frac{1 \times \square}{3 \times \square} = \frac{2}{6}$

2. $\frac{3}{4}$ and $\frac{9}{12}$

$\frac{3}{4} = \frac{3 \times \square}{4 \times \square} = \frac{9}{12}$

3. $\frac{2}{5}$ and $\frac{4}{10}$

$\frac{2}{5} = \frac{2 \times \square}{5 \times \square} = \frac{4}{10}$

4. $\frac{2}{4}$ and $\frac{6}{12}$

$\frac{2}{4} = \frac{2 \times \square}{4 \times \square} = \frac{6}{12}$

Complete to show how the fractions are equivalent.

5. $\frac{5}{6}$ and $\frac{35}{42}$

$\frac{5}{6} = \frac{5 \times \square}{6 \times \square} = \frac{35}{42}$

6. $\frac{4}{7}$ and $\frac{36}{63}$

$\frac{4}{7} = \frac{4 \times \square}{7 \times \square} = \frac{36}{63}$

Complete.

7. $\frac{4}{9} = \frac{4 \times \square}{9 \times \square} = \frac{\square}{45}$

8. $\frac{2}{5} = \frac{2 \times \square}{5 \times \square} = \frac{\square}{40}$

9. $\frac{3}{8} = \frac{3 \times \square}{8 \times \square} = \frac{18}{\square}$

UNIT 6 LESSON 12   Find Equivalent Fractions by Multiplying

6-12 Remembering

Draw the next figure in the pattern.

1.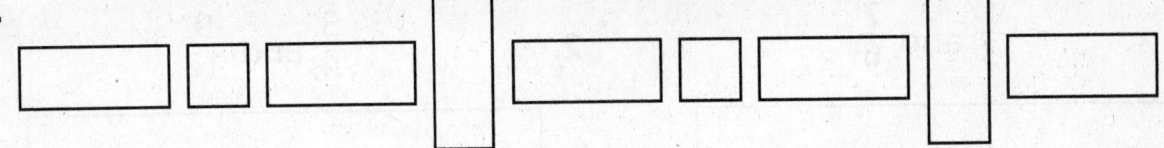

2.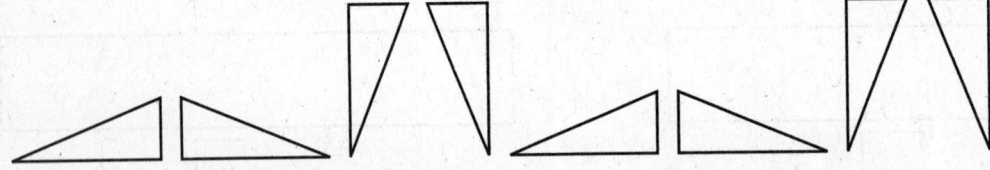

3.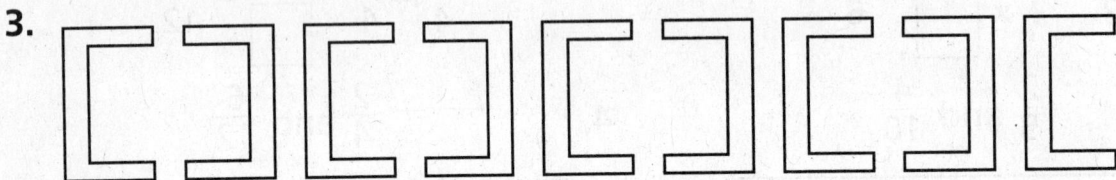

4.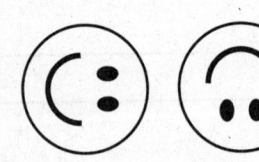

Complete each Missing Number puzzle.

5.

×	6		7
9		72	
	24		28
	18	24	21

6.

×	8		
7		28	63
5	40		45
	24	12	

Find Equivalent Fractions by Multiplying

6-13 Homework

Use grouping to show that the fractions are equivalent.

1. $\dfrac{6}{9}$ and $\dfrac{2}{3}$

2. $\dfrac{9}{12}$ and $\dfrac{3}{4}$

$\dfrac{6}{9} = \dfrac{6 \div \Box}{9 \div \Box} = \dfrac{2}{3}$

$\dfrac{9}{12} = \dfrac{9 \div \Box}{12 \div \Box} = \dfrac{3}{4}$

3. $\dfrac{12}{20}$ and $\dfrac{3}{5}$

4. $\dfrac{16}{24}$ and $\dfrac{2}{3}$

$\dfrac{12}{20} = \dfrac{12 \div \Box}{20 \div \Box} = \dfrac{3}{5}$

$\dfrac{16}{24} = \dfrac{16 \div \Box}{24 \div \Box} = \dfrac{2}{3}$

Simplify.

5. $\dfrac{10}{60} = \dfrac{10 \div \Box}{60 \div \Box} = \dfrac{\Box}{6}$

6. $\dfrac{9}{45} = \dfrac{9 \div \Box}{45 \div \Box} = \dfrac{1}{\Box}$

7. $\dfrac{27}{36} = \dfrac{27 \div \Box}{36 \div \Box} = \dfrac{\Box}{4}$

8. $\dfrac{20}{24} = \dfrac{20 \div \Box}{24 \div \Box} = \dfrac{\Box}{6}$

9. $\dfrac{14}{21} = \dfrac{14 \div \Box}{21 \div \Box} = \dfrac{2}{\Box}$

10. $\dfrac{16}{40} = \dfrac{16 \div \Box}{40 \div \Box} = \dfrac{2}{\Box}$

11. $\dfrac{24}{64} = \dfrac{24 \div \Box}{64 \div \Box} = \dfrac{\Box}{8}$

12. $\dfrac{16}{72} = \dfrac{16 \div \Box}{72 \div \Box} = \dfrac{2}{\Box}$

13. $\dfrac{24}{42} = \dfrac{24 \div \Box}{42 \div \Box} = \dfrac{\Box}{7}$

UNIT 6 LESSON 13 — Find Equivalent Fractions by Dividing

6-13

Remembering

Write each time in numbers. Then write each time in words.

1.

_____

_____

2.

_____

_____

3.

_____

_____

4.

_____

_____

5.

_____

_____

6.

_____

_____

Complete the table.

7.

Start Time	Elapsed Time	End Time
9:05 A.M.		9:55 A.M.
10:30 A.M.	2 hours, 30 minutes	
	4 hours, 30 minutes	3:25 P.M.
7:05 P.M.	5 hours, 15 minutes	
4:25 P.M.		8:30 P.M.
7:10 A.M.	3 hours, 45 minutes	

266 UNIT 6 LESSON 13

Find Equivalent Fractions by Dividing

6-14 Name Date

Homework

Add. Use fraction strips to help if you need to.

1. $\frac{2}{8} + \frac{3}{8} =$ _____

2. $\frac{5}{16} + \frac{3}{16} =$ _____

3. $\frac{3}{7} + \frac{4}{7} =$ _____

4. $\frac{2}{3} + \frac{2}{12} =$ _____

$\frac{\square}{12} + \frac{2}{12} = \frac{\square}{12}$

Add twelfths.

5. $\frac{2}{4} + \frac{3}{12} =$ _____

$\frac{\square}{12} + \frac{3}{12} = \frac{\square}{12}$

Add twelfths.

6. $\frac{3}{10} + \frac{2}{5} =$ _____

$\frac{3}{10} + \frac{\square}{10} = \frac{\square}{10}$

Add tenths.

7. $\frac{1}{3} + \frac{2}{5} =$ _____

$\frac{\square}{15} + \frac{\square}{15} = \frac{\square}{15}$

Add fifteenths.

8. $\frac{2}{4} + \frac{3}{8} =$ _____

Add _____.

9. $\frac{2}{3} + \frac{1}{4} =$ _____

Add _____.

10. $\frac{2}{6} + \frac{2}{4} =$ _____

Add _____.

11. $\frac{3}{9} + \frac{1}{6} =$ _____

Add _____.

12. $\frac{1}{6} + \frac{2}{4} =$ _____

Add _____.

UNIT 6 LESSON 14 Add Any Fractions 267

6–14 Name   Date

Remembering

Write the equivalent fractions shown in the drawing.

1.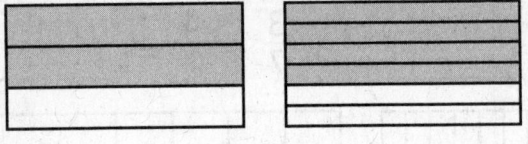

___ = ___

2.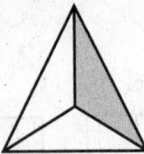

___ = ___

3.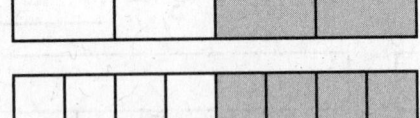

___ = ___

4.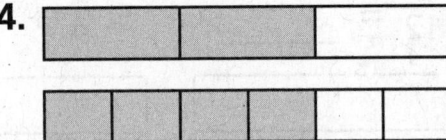

___ = ___

5.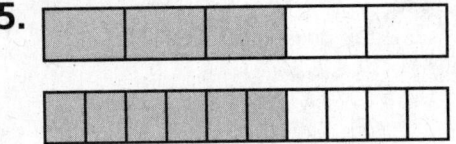

___ = ___

6.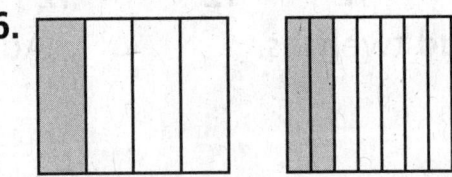

___ = ___

7.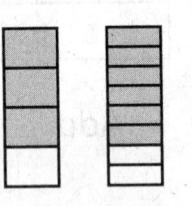

___ = ___

8.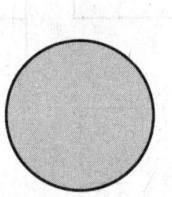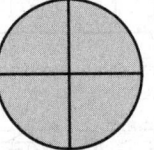

___ = ___

Solve.

9. Jane's mother baked 25 cookies. Jane ate $\frac{2}{5}$ of them. How many did she eat?

10. Ali has 28 math problems. He has finished $\frac{5}{7}$ of them. How many problems has Ali finished?

268 UNIT 6 LESSON 14   Add Any Fractions

6-15 Homework

Compare. Write >, <, or = in the ◯. Use fraction strips if you need to.

1. $\frac{1}{2}$ ◯ $\frac{1}{3}$
2. $\frac{1}{4}$ ◯ $\frac{1}{5}$
3. $\frac{2}{5}$ ◯ $\frac{4}{5}$

4. $\frac{5}{5}$ ◯ $\frac{4}{6}$
5. $\frac{3}{8}$ ◯ $\frac{2}{4}$
6. $\frac{2}{6}$ ◯ $\frac{1}{3}$

Write the fractions in order from greatest to least.

7. $\frac{1}{3}, \frac{1}{6}, \frac{1}{5}$
8. $\frac{2}{6}, \frac{1}{6}, \frac{5}{6}$
9. $\frac{2}{3}, \frac{2}{4}, \frac{2}{5}$

_____   _____   _____

Add, compare, and subtract each pair of fractions.

	Add	Compare	Subtract
10.	$\frac{1}{6} + \frac{1}{3} = $ _____	$\frac{1}{6}$ ◯ $\frac{1}{3}$	
11.	$\frac{2}{5} + \frac{1}{2} = $ _____	$\frac{2}{5}$ ◯ $\frac{1}{2}$	
12.	$\frac{3}{8} + \frac{1}{8} = $ _____	$\frac{3}{8}$ ◯ $\frac{1}{8}$	

Solve.

13. In Kayla's marble collection, $\frac{1}{4}$ of the marbles are blue and $\frac{3}{8}$ are red. Are there more blue marbles or red marbles? Explain.

_____

UNIT 6 LESSON 15   Compare and Subtract Fractions **269**

6–15

Remembering

Multiply or divide.

1. 49 ÷ 7 = ☐

2. 42 / 6 = ☐

3. 8)̄56

4. 8 × 7 = ☐

5. 6 × 6 = ☐

6. 48 ÷ 8 = ☐

7. 7)̄42

8. 72 ÷ 8 = ☐

9. 6 * 8 = ☐

10. 7 • 6 = ☐

11. 8)̄72

12. 36 / 6 = ☐

Mark all the words that describe each triangle.

13.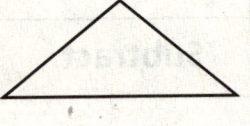

☐ equilateral
☐ isosceles
☐ scalene
☐ right
☐ acute
☐ obtuse

14.

☐ equilateral
☐ isosceles
☐ scalene
☐ right
☐ acute
☐ obtuse

15.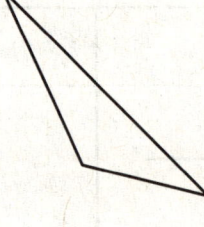

☐ equilateral
☐ isosceles
☐ scalene
☐ right
☐ acute
☐ obtuse

16.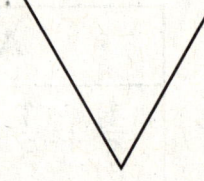

☐ equilateral
☐ isosceles
☐ scalene
☐ right
☐ acute
☐ obtuse

Compare and Subtract Fractions

6–16 Name _____ Date _____

Homework

Circle a length to show each fraction. Then compare them using >, <, or =.

1. $\frac{1}{2} \bigcirc \frac{3}{6}$

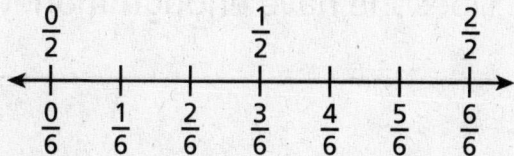

2. $\frac{2}{5} \bigcirc \frac{2}{10}$

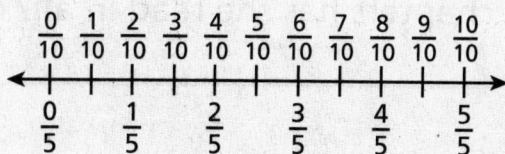

Circle the lengths to add or subtract.

3. $\frac{1}{6} + \frac{3}{6} = $ _____

4. $\frac{5}{6} - \frac{3}{6} = $ _____

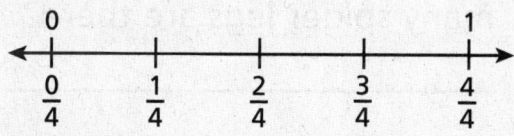
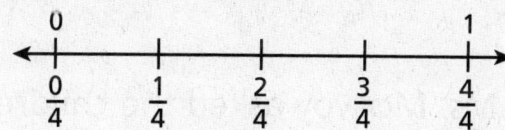

5. $\frac{1}{4} + \frac{3}{4} = $ _____

6. $\frac{3}{4} - \frac{2}{4} = $ _____

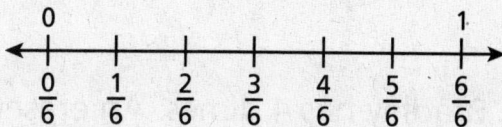

Write each fraction as a decimal.

7. $\frac{2}{10} = $ _____

8. $\frac{8}{100} = $ _____

9. $\frac{75}{100} = $ _____

Write each decimal as a fraction.

10. $0.9 = $ _____

11. $0.3 = $ _____

12. $0.35 = $ _____

Remembering

Solve.

1. Grace has read 2 chapters in each of her 9 books. How many chapters has she read in all?

2. Lehie has 9 nickels. She wants to buy an apple that costs $0.40. Does she have enough money?

3. Hani wrote a letter to each of his 10 friends. Each letter was 3 pages long. How many pages did Hani write?

4. Eric had 2 picnic baskets. He put 7 apples into each basket. How many apples in all did he put into the picnic baskets?

5. Bradley has 4 dimes. An eraser costs a quarter. Does he have enough money?

6. Mai has captured 9 spiders for a school project. Her little sister wonders how many spider legs are in Mai's collection. How many spider legs are there?

7. Ms. McAvoy asked the children in her class to raise their hands if they had exactly 3 pets. Seven children raised their hands. How many pets do these 7 children have altogether?

8. Music and Video Express had a sale. Kate bought 2 videos for $5.98 each and headphones for $7.99. She gave the cashier a $20 bill. How much change should she get?

9. How many wheels do 8 cars have?

10. How many legs do 6 rabbits have?

Fractions on a Number Line

6–17 Homework

Write the mixed number and improper fraction that each drawing shows.

1.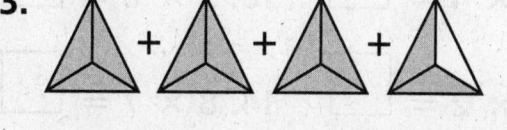

   1 + ___ = ___

   $\frac{4}{4}$ + ___ = ___

2.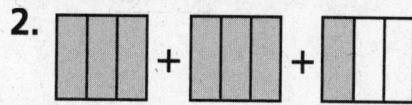

   1 + ___ + ___ = ___

   $\frac{3}{3}$ + ___ + ___ = ___

3.

   1 + ___ + ___ + ___ = ___

   $\frac{3}{3}$ + ___ + ___ + ___ = ___

4.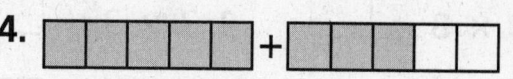

   1 + ___ = ___

   ___ + ___ = ___

Write the improper fraction or mixed number.

5. $\frac{13}{7}$ = $\frac{7}{7} + \frac{6}{7} = 1\frac{6}{7}$

6. $1\frac{2}{5}$ = $\frac{5}{5} + \frac{2}{5} = \frac{7}{5}$

7. $\frac{8}{3}$ = _____

8. $2\frac{3}{7}$ = _____

9. $\frac{13}{5}$ = _____

10. $3\frac{5}{9}$ = _____

11. $\frac{19}{4}$ = _____

12. $2\frac{1}{6}$ = _____

UNIT 6 LESSON 17 — Improper Fractions and Mixed Numbers 273

Remembering

Add or subtract.

1. $1.14
   + 3.67

2. 192
   + 479

3. 518
   − 371

4. $5.52
   + 4.48

5. $4.44 − $1.81 = _____

6. 724 − 68 = _____

Multiply or divide.

7. 9 × 8 = ☐
8. 7 × 3 = ☐
9. 4 × 4 = ☐
10. 5 × 8 = ☐
11. 6 × 3 = ☐
12. 4 × 7 = ☐
13. 9 × 2 = ☐
14. 8 × 7 = ☐

Solve.

15. Elijah had $20. He spent $\frac{1}{2}$ of the money on paint and $\frac{1}{4}$ of it on art paper. How much money does he have left

_____

16. James ate $\frac{3}{8}$ of a pizza. Joyce ate $\frac{1}{4}$ of the pizza. What fraction of the pizza did they eat together?

_____

17. Chaka drank $\frac{3}{4}$ of a glass of lemonade. Shana drank $\frac{7}{8}$ of a glass of lemonade. Who drank more lemonade? How much more?

_____

18. There was a party in Mr. Spector's class. Jonelle brought $\frac{1}{2}$ of the cookies and Raya brought $\frac{1}{3}$ of the cookies. Who brought more cookies?

_____

6–18

Homework

Write the answer.

1. 6)44   2. 4)29   3. 5)42   4. 9)47

5. 7)59   6. 4)34   7. 7)63   8. 9)57

9. 8)70   10. 4)28   11. 7)67   12. 6)40

Solve.

13. Gus is making valentines. He needs 6 paper hearts for each one. He has 55 hearts. How many valentines can he make? How many paper hearts will be left over?

14. Felipe is gathering the soccer balls after the team's practice. There are 32 balls. Each sack holds 7 balls. How many sacks does Felipe need to gather all the balls?

15. Ashley is putting ice cubes into glasses before dinner. There are 46 ice cubes. Each glass holds 6 ice cubes. How many glasses can she fill completely? How many ice cubes will be left over?

16. The Outdoor Club is planning a canoe trip. There are 31 people in the club. Each canoe can hold 4 people. How many canoes does the club need to rent for the trip?

Remembering

6–18

Add, compare, and subtract each pair of fractions.

	Add	Compare	Subtract
1.	$\frac{1}{6} + \frac{3}{4} =$ _____	$\frac{1}{6} \bigcirc \frac{3}{4}$	
2.	$\frac{2}{8} + \frac{1}{4} =$ _____	$\frac{2}{8} \bigcirc \frac{1}{4}$	
3.	$\frac{3}{7} + \frac{1}{2} =$ _____	$\frac{3}{7} \bigcirc \frac{1}{2}$	
4.	$\frac{4}{5} + \frac{1}{10} =$ _____	$\frac{4}{5} \bigcirc \frac{1}{10}$	
5.	$\frac{1}{3} + \frac{3}{8} =$ _____	$\frac{1}{3} \bigcirc \frac{3}{8}$	

Find the area of each figure.

6.

7.

6-19 Homework

Write the quotient with a remainder or as a mixed number.

1. 7)37   2. 8)78   3. 6)49   4. 3)19

5. 7)52   6. 6)54   7. 7)67   8. 8)70

9. 6)40   10. 9)38   11. 8)64   12. 7)25

Solve.

13. The third-graders at Coburn School won a recycling contest. The 4 third-grade classes get to share 38 pizzas equally. How much pizza does each class get?

14. David has 70 cans of paint to pack into crates. Each crate holds 8 cans of paint. How many crates will David need to pack all the paint?

15. Mabel has 45 stickers. She can fit 10 stickers on each page. How many pages will she fill completely? How many stickers will be left?

16. The 8 soccer players of the Middle School soccer team will share 20 bottles of water equally. How much water will each player get?

UNIT 6 LESSON 19   Understand Remainders

6-19 Remembering

Find the missing number.

1. $56 \div 7 = \square$
2. $7 * \square = 63$
3. $3\overline{)\square}$ with 12 on top
4. $81 \div \square = 9$
5. $\square\overline{)48}$ with 6 on top
6. $4 \cdot 7 = \square$
7. $4\overline{)32}$ with $\square$ on top
8. $72 \div \square = 9$
9. $\square \times 4 = 12$
10. $\square \div 6 = 4$
11. $6 \times \square = 12$
12. $56 / \square = 8$

Find the measure of the unknown angle.

13.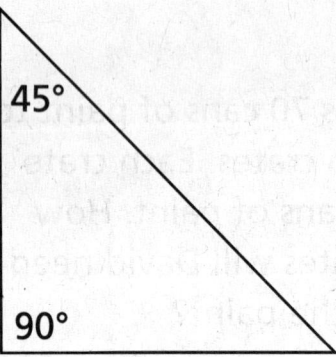

14.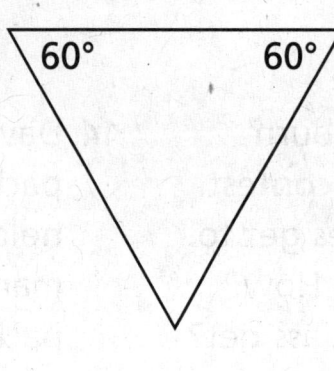

15.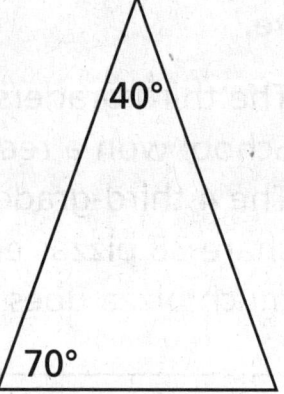

16. Jonathan has $\frac{1}{5}$ as many markers as Sheila. Sheila has 25 markers. How many markers does Jonathan have?

17. The Tigers won 20 baseball games this season. The Hawks won $\frac{3}{4}$ as many games. How many games did the Hawks win?

278 UNIT 6 LESSON 19 — Understand Remainders

6-20 Homework

Write the answer with a remainder and as a mixed number.

1. 68 ÷ 8 _____

2. 41 ÷ 7 _____

3. 82 ÷ 9 _____

4. 38 ÷ 4 _____

5. 57 ÷ 7 _____

6. 78 ÷ 8 _____

7. 49 ÷ 8 _____

8. 40 ÷ 6 _____

Solve.

9. Emma's father is building her a dollhouse. Each room can hold 6 dolls. If Emma has 38 dolls, how many rooms does her father need to build in the doll house?

10. Mamie is baking cupcakes for her 7 cousins. She wants to divide the cupcakes equally among her cousins. If Mamie bakes 45 cupcakes, how many whole cupcakes will each cousin get? What part of a cupcake will each cousin get?

11. Monica has 39 pieces of tape. She needs 4 pieces to hang 1 poster. How many posters can she hang? How many pieces of tape will she have left over?

12. Mr. Chavez made 19 pies for his 4 neighbors. If the neighbors share the pies equally, how much pie will each neighbor get?

UNIT 6 LESSON 20 — Practice Division with Remainders **279**

6-20 Remembering

Solve.

1. Betty and Jake hit baseballs at the batting cage. Betty's first hit flew 81 feet. Jake's ball went $\frac{1}{9}$ as far. How many feet did Jake's ball travel?

   _____

2. Roberto and Jayla weighed some candy. Roberto had 6 pounds, and Jayla had $\frac{2}{3}$ as much. How many pounds of candy did Jayla have?

   _____

3. Tyrone bought a sweater that cost $26.99. Then he bought a coat that cost twice as much. How much did he spend in all?

   _____

4. A carpenter has two screws. One is $\frac{1}{2}$ inch long and the other is $\frac{7}{8}$ inch long. How much longer is one screw than the other?

   _____

Which two figures in each row are congruent?

5.        _____

6. 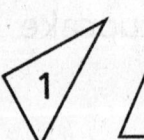 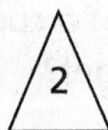 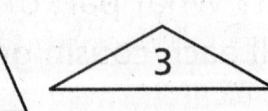 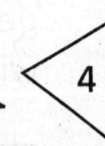 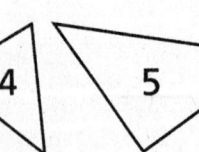   _____

7.   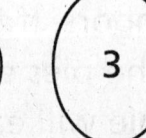 (5)   _____

Practice Division with Remainders

F-1 Homework

Circle the nets you predict will form a cube. Use extra paper to draw and test one of your predictions.

1.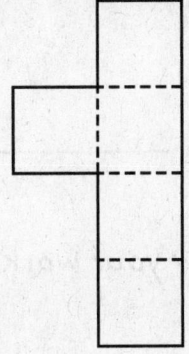

2.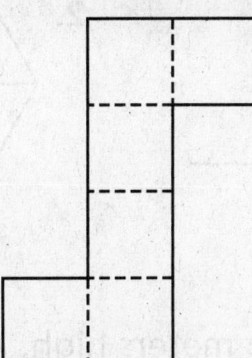

3.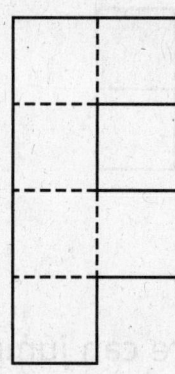

4.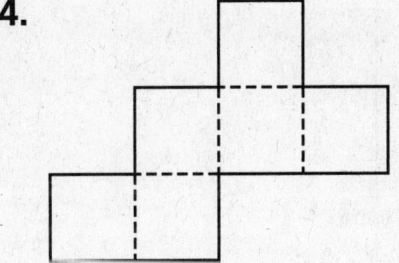

5.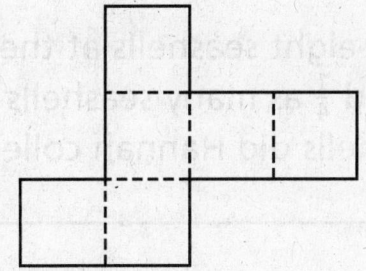

6.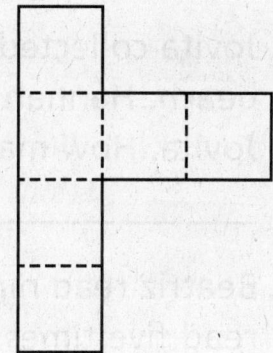

7. On grid paper, draw a different net that will form a cube when it is cut out and folded.

UNIT F LESSON 1   Explore Cubes **281**

F-1 Name _____ Date _____

Remembering

Write a fraction to represent the shaded portion of the figure.

1. 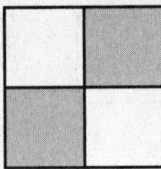 _____

2.  _____

Solve.   Show your work.

3. A hare can jump about two meters high. A tiger can jump twice as high. How many meters high can a tiger jump?

   _____

4. Jovita collected twenty-eight seashells at the beach. Hannah collected $\frac{1}{4}$ as many seashells as Jovita. How many seashells did Hannah collect?

   _____

5. Beatriz read nine books over the summer. Jared read five times as many books as Beatriz. How many books did Jared read?

   _____

Write the time in numbers and write two ways to say the time.

6.

7.

8.

_____   _____   _____

_____   _____   _____

282 UNIT F LESSON 1   Explore Cubes

F-2 Homework

Name _____ Date _____

Use the model for exercises 1–2.

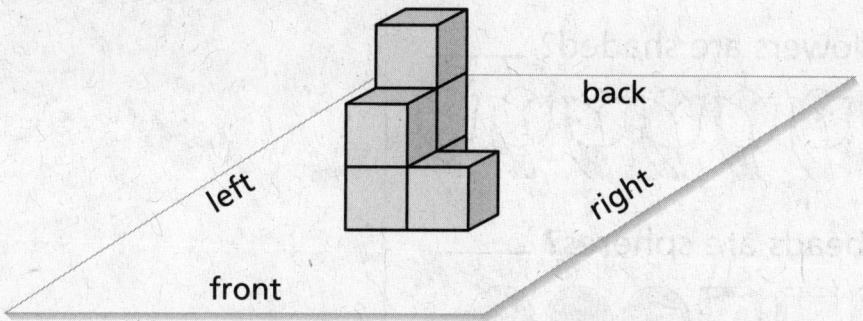

1. Draw the top view of the model.

2. Label each view of the model as *front, back, right,* or *left*.

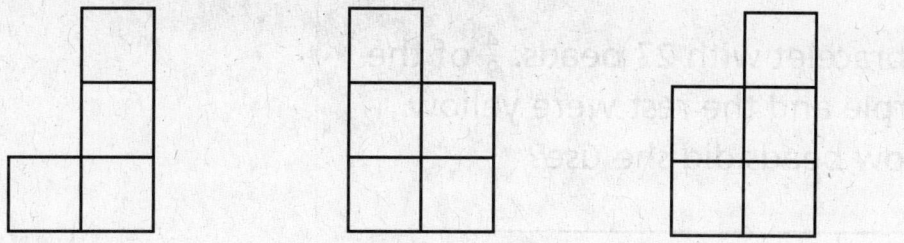

_____   _____   _____   _____

Use the model below for exercise 3.

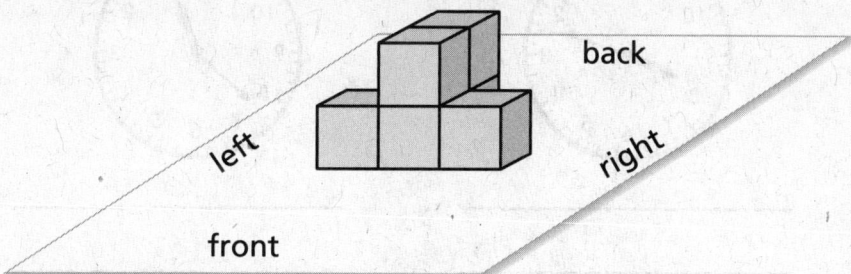

3. Draw the *front, back, right,* and *left* views of the model.

    front   back   left   right

UNIT F LESSON 2 — Two-Dimensional Pictures of Three-Dimensional Buildings **283**

F-2 Remembering

Solve. *Show your work.*

1. What fraction of the flowers are shaded? _____

2. What fraction of the beads are spheres? _____

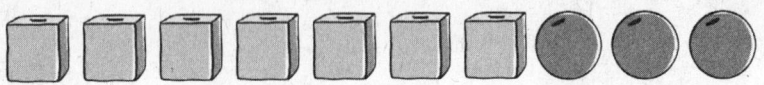

3. Mitchell built 15 cars from blocks. He put wheels on $\frac{2}{5}$ of them. On how many cars did he put wheels?

_____

4. Eileen made a bracelet with 27 beads. $\frac{4}{9}$ of the beads were purple and the rest were yellow. How many yellow beads did she use?

_____

Write the time in numbers. Then write two ways to say the time.

5.

_____
_____
_____

6.

_____
_____
_____

7.

_____
_____
_____

Write the time in numbers.

8. twelve past six

_____

9. seven twenty-four

_____

F-3 Homework

Name the solid figure. List some real-world items that have the same shape.

1.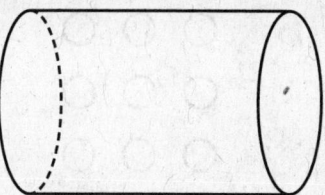

_____
_____
_____

2.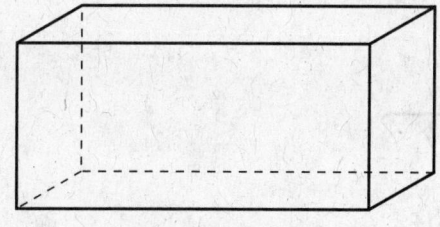

_____
_____
_____

3.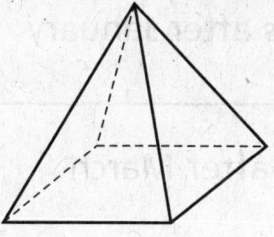

_____
_____
_____

UNIT F LESSON 3   Explore Prisms, Cylinders, and Pyramids **285**

F-3 Remembering

Shade the given fraction.

1. $\frac{3}{4}$

2. $\frac{5}{7}$

3. $\frac{5}{9}$

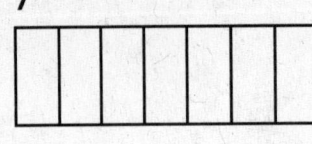

Solve.

4. There are 56 horses on a farm. One eighth of them are in the barn. How many horses are in the barn?

   _____

5. One sixth of the books on Alan's shelf are about Egypt. There are 24 books on the shelf. How many books on the shelf are about Egypt?

   _____

Find the month.

6. Three months after April

   _____

7. Three months after January

   _____

8. Seven months after May

   _____

9. Nine months after March

   _____

10. Two months after December

    _____

11. Four months before August

    _____

286 UNIT F LESSON 3   Explore Prisms, Cylinders, and Pyramids

F-4 Homework

Name each solid figure. Write other things that are this shape.

1.

_____
_____

2.

_____
_____

3.

_____
_____

Draw the shape of a package you could use to ship a telescope.

4.

Remembering F–4

Use mental math.

1. $\frac{1}{4} \times 4 =$ _____
2. $\frac{1}{2} \times 8 =$ _____
3. $\frac{1}{3} \times 12 =$ _____

Write each equation two other ways.

4. $\frac{1}{4}$ of $12 = 3$

   _____

   _____

5. $16 \div 4 = 4$

   _____

   _____

6. $\frac{3}{7} \times 21 = 9$

   _____

   _____

Solve. *Show your work.*

7. Vanya organized 27 photos into an album. Four photos fit on each page. How many pages did she use? How many photos were on the page that was not full?

   _____

8. Michel had 38 marbles. He gave 9 marbles to each player. How many players were there? How many marbles were left over?

   _____

Write the time as minutes after an hour and minutes before an hour.

9.

   _____

10.

    _____

11.

    _____

288 UNIT F LESSON 4 Explore Cones

F-5 Homework

1. Place a pencil inside one end of a large paper clip. Hold the pencil point in place on this sheet of paper. Place another pencil inside the other end of the paper clip. Ask your Homework Helper to hold your paper still while you draw a circle by moving the second pencil. Label one radius, one diameter, and the circumference.

2. Name three spheres that you might see every day.
   _____

3. Give one example of how a sphere is similar to a circle.
   _____

4. Give one example of how a sphere is different from a circle.
   _____

UNIT F LESSON 5 — Explore Circles and Spheres

Remembering

Solve.

1. How many fourths are in one half? _____

2. _____ fourths = 1 half

3. $\frac{\square}{4} = \frac{1}{2}$

4. How many twelfths are in one third? _____

5. _____ twelfths = 1 third

6. $\frac{\square}{12} = \frac{1}{3}$

Solve.

Show your work.

7. A chef is preparing meals for 8 dinner guests. She has cooked 32 small potatoes. Each plate will have an equal number of potatoes. How many potatoes will she put on each plate?

_____

9. A pastry chef is making blackberry pies and a blackberry crumble. He has nineteen cups of blackberries. Each pie uses three cups of blackberries. If he makes five pies, how many cups of blackberries will he have for the crumble?

_____

Fill in the blanks.

9. From 6:36 to 6:51, _____ minutes pass, and the minute hand rotates _____ degrees.

10. From 6:15 to 6:45, _____ minutes pass, and the minute hand rotates _____ degrees.

7-3 Homework

Estimate the length of each line segment. Then measure it to the nearest centimeter.

1. ———————————
   Estimate: _____ Actual: _____

|———| 1 centimeter

2. ——————
   Estimate: _____ Actual: _____

3. ————————
   Estimate: _____ Actual: _____

Complete the tables.

4.
m	cm
1	
2	
	500
8	
10	

5.
m	dm
1	
	50
	60
8	
9	

6.
dm	m
10	
20	
40	
	8
	10

7. Describe a distance that is about 3 meters long.

_____

Choose the unit you would use to measure each. Write *centimeter*, *decimeter*, *meter*, or *kilometer*.

8. the height of a chair _____

9. the distance you can throw a ball _____

10. the distance you could walk in half an hour _____

UNIT 7 LESSON 3 — Centimeters, Decimeters, and Meters

7-3 Remembering

Use the graph to answer the questions below.

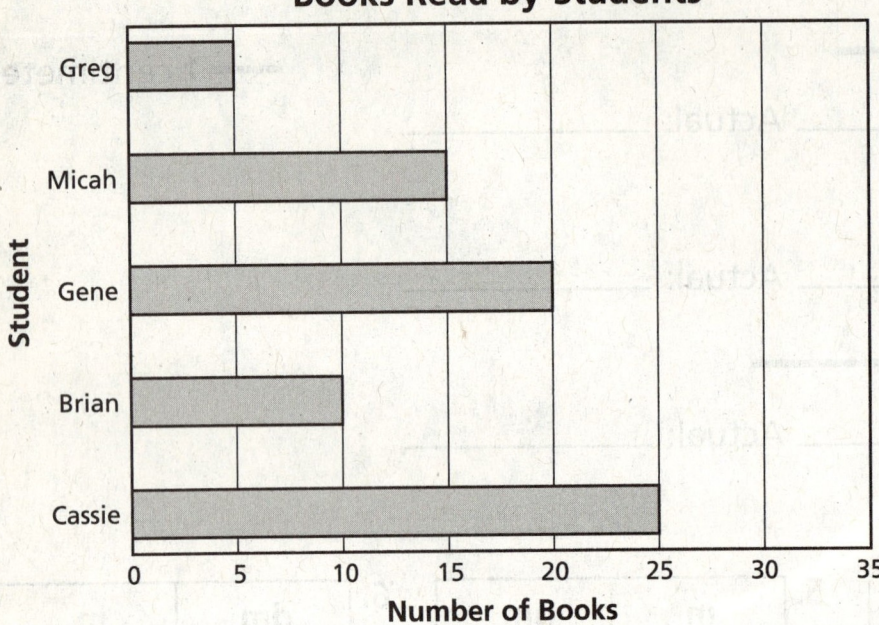

1. Micah read _____ as many books as Greg.

   Greg read _____ as many books as Micah.

2. Cassie read _____ as many books as Greg.

   Greg read _____ as many books as Cassie.

3. Gene read _____ as many books as Brian.

   Brian read _____ as many books as Gene.

Solve.

4. Julia wants to give some books to 6 of her friends. She has 38 books to give away. How many books will each friend receive? How many books will be left over?

   _____

5. A grocer is packing oranges into boxes of 10. If he has 98 oranges, how many boxes will he need to pack all the oranges? _____

7-4 Homework

Estimate the perimeter in inches. Then measure each side to the nearest $\frac{1}{4}$ inch and find the perimeter.

1.

Estimate: _____

Actual: _____

2.

Estimate: _____

Actual: _____

Add.

3. $2\frac{1}{4}$ inches + 1 inches

   _____

4. $5\frac{2}{4}$ inches + $\frac{1}{4}$ inches

   _____

5. $1\frac{1}{2}$ inches + $8\frac{1}{4}$ inches

   _____

6. $4\frac{1}{4}$ inches + $1\frac{3}{4}$ inches

   _____

7. $\frac{1}{2}$ inches + $\frac{3}{4}$ inches

   _____

8. $2\frac{1}{2}$ inches + $3\frac{1}{2}$ inches

   _____

Solve.

9. Todd wants to buy ribbon to go around the edge of the sign below. How many inches of ribbon should he buy?

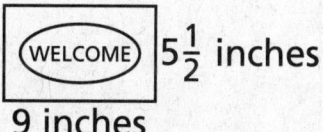

$5\frac{1}{2}$ inches

9 inches

_____

10. Marie needs 15 inches of yarn to make a project. She has the yarn shown below. Does she have enough yarn? Explain.

$9\frac{1}{2}$ inches $4\frac{1}{2}$ inches

_____

UNIT 7 LESSON 4   Add Lengths **297**

7-4 Remembering

1 foot (ft) = 12 inches (in.)
1 yard (yd) = 3 ft or 36 in.

Complete.

1. 1 feet 5 inches = _____ inches
2. 2 yards 1 foot = _____ feet
3. 2 feet 5 inches = _____ inches
4. 5 yards 2 feet = _____ feet
5. 30 feet = _____ yards
6. 9 feet = _____ yards
7. 19 feet = _____ yards _____ foot
8. 31 feet = _____ yards _____ foot
9. 26 feet = _____ yards
10. 17 feet = _____ yards

Solve.

Show your work.

11. Saundra has 37 inches of blue thread. She needs 4 inches of thread for each button she wants to sew on her shirt. How many buttons can Saundra sew on? How many inches of thread will be left over?

12. Ms. Pons has 78 feet of yarn for her class. She wants to divide it equally among her 8 students. How much yarn can each student have?

13. Mary has 46 yards of string. She needs 6 yards of string to mark off each of her flower beds. How many flower beds can Mary mark off? How much string will be left over?

298 UNIT 7 LESSON 4

Add Lengths

7-7 Homework

Write the improper fraction or mixed number.

1. $\frac{6}{4}$ c = _____ c
2. $\frac{8}{6}$ ft = _____ ft
3. $\frac{12}{7}$ qt = ___ qt
4. $1\frac{5}{6}$ ft = ___ ft
5. $1\frac{1}{3}$ c = ___ c
6. $2\frac{1}{5}$ gal = ___ gal
7. $\frac{10}{3}$ gal = ___ gal
8. $\frac{12}{5}$ yd = ___ yd
9. $1\frac{5}{6}$ ft = ___ ft
10. $\frac{8}{5}$ mi = ___ mi
11. $\frac{5}{3}$ c = ___ c
12. $2\frac{4}{7}$ mi = ___ mi
13. $\frac{15}{12}$ ft = _____ ft
14. $7\frac{2}{3}$ yd = ___ yd
15. $4\frac{3}{4}$ ft = ___ ft

Write the length of each line segment using an improper fraction and a mixed number.

16. _____

17. _____

18. _____

7-7 Remembering

Divide. If there is a remainder, give the answer as a mixed number.

1. 54 / 2 _____
2. 82 ÷ 4 _____
3. 30 ÷ 6 _____
4. 24 ÷ 12 _____
5. 58 ÷ 3 _____
6. 45 / 7 _____
7. 73 ÷ 8 _____
8. 36 / 3 _____
9. 43 / 9 _____
10. 19 ÷ 2 _____
11. 37 ÷ 5 _____
12. 48 / 2 _____

Solve.

13. At the right is a diagram of George's rock garden. He wants to put a fence around it. How much fencing does he need? The fencing costs $10 per foot. Use mental math to find the total cost.

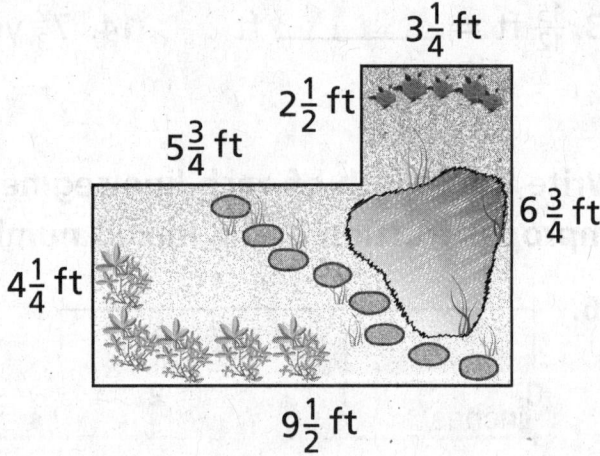

14. Mrs. Lee wants to put tile on the floor of her kitchen. Each tile covers 1 square foot. How many tiles does she need to cover the floor? Each tile costs $3. Use mental math to find the total cost.

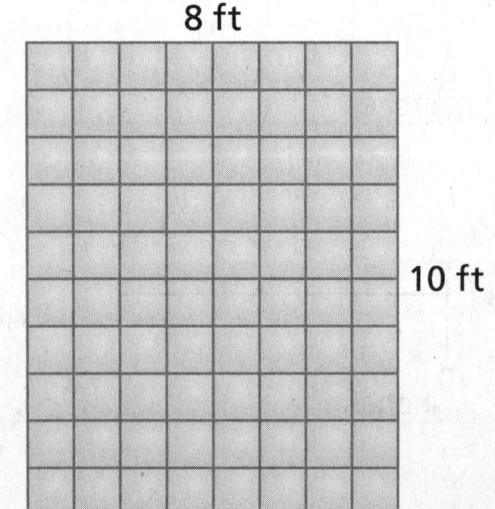

304 UNIT 7 LESSON 7 — Improper Fractions and Mixed Numbers in Measurements

7-9 Homework

Choose the unit you would use to measure the weight of each object. Write *ounce* or *pound*.

1.

2.

3.

_____   _____   _____

Choose the unit you would use to measure the mass of each object. Write *gram* or *kilogram*.

4.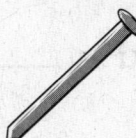

5.

6.

_____   _____   _____

Circle the better estimate.

7. a pillow   8 oz   8 lb   8. a stapler   250 g   250 kg
9. a car   1,000 g   1,000 kg   10. a large book   3 lb   30 lb

Complete.

11.
Ounces	16	2			12
Pounds	1		$\frac{4}{16}$ or $\frac{1}{4}$	2	$\frac{1}{2}$

12.
Grams	1,000		3,000			5
Kilograms	1	$\frac{3}{1,000}$		5	$\frac{1}{2}$	

Solve.

13. Michael has 1 pound of ground turkey to make 4 turkey burgers of the same weight. How many ounces should he put in each turkey burger?

_____

Remembering

Complete.

1. $1\frac{1}{2}$ in. + $3\frac{6}{8}$ in.

   _____

2. $7\frac{3}{4}$ in. + $\frac{3}{8}$ in.

   _____

3. $3\frac{1}{4}$ in. + $7\frac{3}{8}$ in.

   _____

4. $4\frac{3}{4}$ in. + $7\frac{1}{2}$ in.

   _____

Complete.

5. 13 ft = _____ yd

6. 13 ft = _____ in.

7. 8 yd = _____ ft

8. 20 cm = _____ dm

9. 20 dm = _____ m

10. 4 m = _____ cm

11. 11 pt = _____ qt

12. 7 qt = _____ gal

13. 4 c = _____ fl oz

14. 8 L = _____ mL

15. 750 mL = _____ L

16. 5,500 mL = _____ L

Complete the table.

17.

Start Time	Elapsed Time	End Time
10:05 A.M.		10:55 P.M.
11:30 A.M.	2 hours, 30 minutes	
	4 hours, 30 minutes	2:15 P.M.
8:25 P.M.	5 hours, 15 minutes	

308 UNIT 7 LESSON 9 — Customary Units of Weight and Metric Units of Mass

G-1 Homework

This is a map of the animals in a zoo.

1. If you start at the entrance and walk 3 units up and 3 units left, where will you be? _____

2. Which is closer to the koala, the kangaroo or the fruit bats? _____

3. Describe a route from the fruit bats to the wallaby.
   _____

4. Choose two places on the map. Describe two routes from one place to the other. Which route is longer?
   _____
   _____

UNIT G LESSON 1   Directions and Maps **311**

Remembering

1. Draw a horizontal line segment that is 4 inches long.

2. Draw a horizontal line segment that is 2 inches long.

Complete.

3. 3 ft = _____ in.
4. 4 yd = _____ ft
5. 24 in. = _____ ft
6. 6 yd = _____ ft
7. 36 in. = _____ ft
8. 7 ft = _____ in.

Solve.

9. A rectangular picture is 4 inches by 7 inches. Elmore has 2 feet of ribbon to go around the picture. Does he have enough ribbon?

   _____

10. A square room has a length of 12 feet. Daniel wants to put new baseboard around the room. How many yards of baseboard does he need?

    _____

Circle the nets that you think will form a cube when folded. Copy the nets onto paper and cut them out. Fold them to test your predictions.

11. 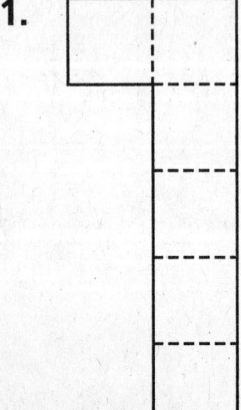   12. 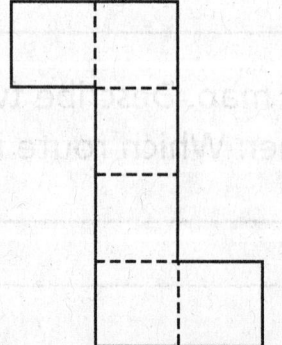   13.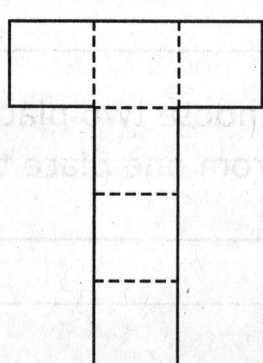

G-2 Homework

Use the coordinate grid below for exercises 1–10.

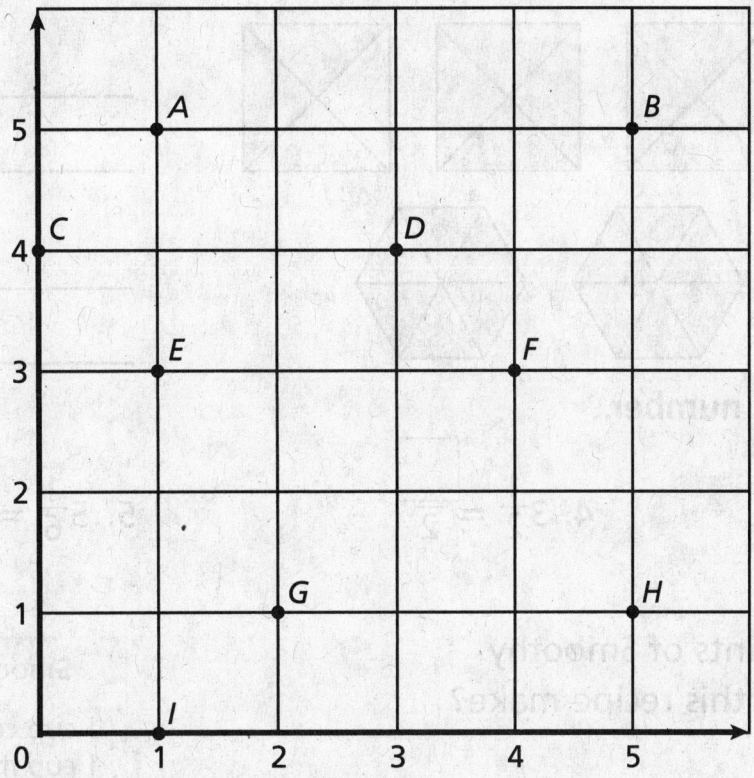

Write the ordered pair for each point.

1. E (____, ____)
2. H (____, ____)
3. G (____, ____)
4. B (____, ____)

Write the letter of the point for each ordered pair.

5. (1, 0) _____
6. (4, 3) _____
7. (3, 4) _____
8. (1, 5) _____
9. (0, 4) _____
10. (5, 1) _____

11. Mark the following ordered pairs on the grid.
    (1, 1) (1, 4) (4, 1) (4, 4)

12. Draw a line segment to connect the points in order that you marked for exercise 11. Name the figure.

_____

UNIT G LESSON 2 — Locate Points on a Coordinate Grid **313**

G-2 Remembering

Write an improper fraction and a mixed number for the shaded part.

1.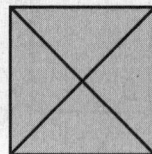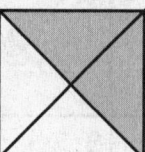

   _____
   _____

2.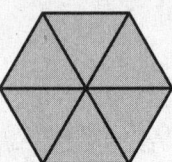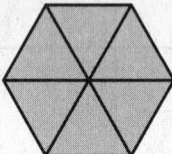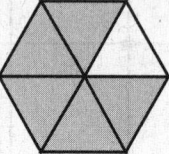

   _____
   _____

Find the missing number.

3. $2\frac{1}{6} = \frac{\square}{6}$

4. $3\frac{1}{2} = \frac{\square}{2}$

5. $5\frac{1}{6} = \frac{\square}{\square}$

Solve.

6. How many pints of Smoothy Delight does this recipe make?

   _____

7. Jill has a 12-cup punch bowl. How many quarts will it hold?

   _____

Smoothy Delight

1 cup crushed ice
1 cup mashed banana
2 cups peach juice
1 cup rice milk

Complete.

8. Name the solid figure shown at the right.

   _____

9. Sketch a net that will make this solid.

10. List three objects in the shape of this solid.

    _____

314 UNIT G LESSON 2   Locate Points on a Coordinate Grid

G-3 Homework

1. Mark a point on this coordinate grid to form the third vertex of an acute triangle.

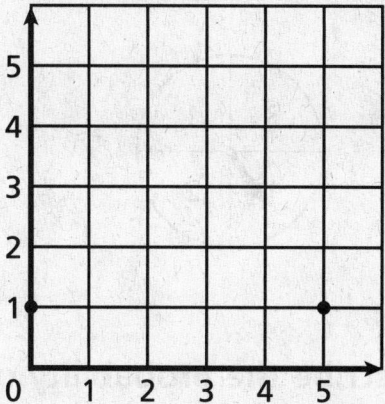

2. Write the ordered pair for each vertex.

   (____, ____) (____, ____) (____, ____)

3. Mark a point on this coordinate grid to form the fourth vertex of a parallelogram. Join the four points to make a parallelogram.

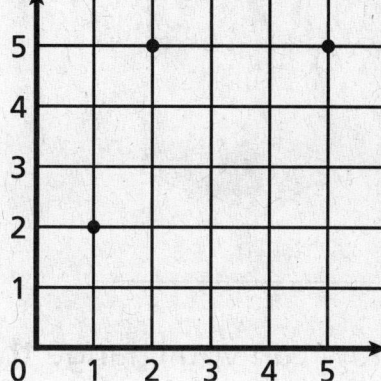

4. Write the ordered pair for each vertex.

   (____, ____) (____, ____)

   (____, ____) (____, ____)

5. Draw a rectangle on this coordinate grid with a width that is 2 units shorter than its length.

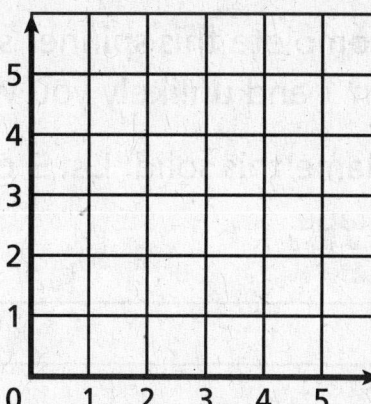

6. Write the ordered pair for each vertex.

   (____, ____) (____, ____)

   (____, ____) (____, ____)

UNIT G LESSON 3   Explore Line Segments and Figures on a Coordinate Grid **315**

Remembering

Which number are you most likely to spin?

1.

　_____

2.

　_____

3.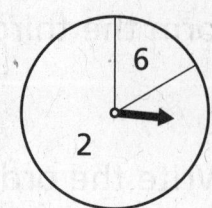

　_____

Describe the probability of picking a black cube.
Use the words *certain*, *likely*, *unlikely*, or *impossible*.

4.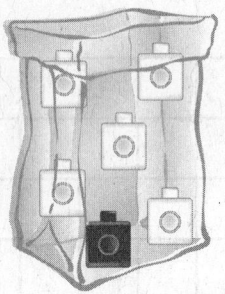

　_____

5.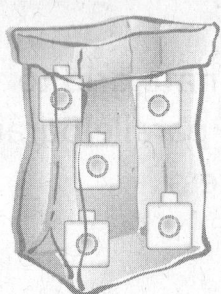

　_____

6.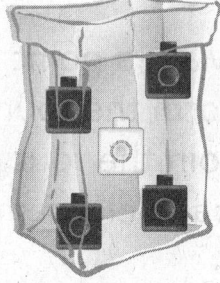

　_____

7. How can you change this spinner to make it certain to land on gray?

   _____
   _____

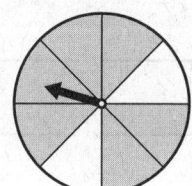

8. Complete this spinner so that it is likely you will land on 1 and unlikely you will land on 2.

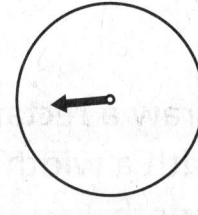

9. Name this solid. List 3 objects that have the same shape.

   _____
   _____

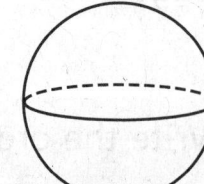